The Sky is Green

AND

the Grass is Blue

THE SKY IS GREEN

——AND——

THE GRASS IS BLUE

TURNING YOUR UPSIDE DOWN WORLD RIGHT SIDE UP!

DEB SCOTT

authorHOUSE®

AuthorHouse™
1663 Liberty Drive
Bloomington, IN 47403
www.authorhouse.com
Phone: 1-800-839-8640

First published by AuthorHouse   12/8/2009

ISBN: 978-1-4490-4479-4 (sc)
ISBN: 978-1-4490-4478-7 (hc)

Printed in the United States of America
Bloomington, Indiana

This book is printed on acid-free paper.

This book is dedicated to my mother, and best friend, Rachel.

I kept my promise mom!

Love Always,

Deb

CONTENTS

Chapter I

You Don't Know, What You Don't Know

Have you? Were you? Did you?

- Grow up in a dysfunctional family?
- Suffered a period of depression or hopelessness?
- Been betrayed by someone you trusted and loved?
- Experienced sexual abuse by a person in authority?
- Battled a fight against alcohol yourself or with a loved one?
- Questioned the existence of God?
- Asked why bad things were happening to you?
- Suffered more than you felt you could bear?
- Experienced the grief of family death?
- Lost all your financial life savings?
- Want to be happy?

If you answered yes to any of the above questions, then I am just like you.

That's good news. Why?

Because you can transform all those perceived negatives into a diamond you love. I am living proof, and if I can do it, so can you!

Don't believe the lie that it is impossible to be happy if you have a history of suffering any kind of tragedy. Don't believe the lie that transformation is impossible. Don't believe the lie that you can't be happy with all these perceived imperfections in your life story. Don't believe the lies! Believe EVERYTHING you now define as bad in your life, CAN and WILL be transformed into something GOOD. They will become unexpected gifts for you to appreciate, and treasure, with continuous happy gratitude.

One of the most important historical events of our time was when Neil Armstrong landed on the moon. How did he get there? In a rocket that was on course only 2.5% of the time! But he still made it to the moon, because the rocket and other pilots were open and willing, and accepted that they had to keep adjusting course along the way to arrive at their final destination. The goal and outcome of that goal was important enough for them to be humbly flexible and willing to adjust rocket settings. They didn't wait until they were 40% off course to get back on the correct coordinates.

What got them there then?

They had the skill set, equipment, and tools to readjust their direction quickly, and so will you. That's what you'll learn here –

the skills to maintain and readjust your course to arrive at your well deserved destination of healthy happiness.

With a million self help, recovery, and motivational books on the shelves, why should you read this one?

What could possibly be different about *The Sky is Green and the Grass is Blue*? How will reading this particular book truly change "my" life?

I often asked myself these types of questions when I wandered through the shelves of books I'd grab to buy and devour when I first began this initial quest for these exact same answers in my own life. It is now my honor and privilege to pass on this knowledge to you. To transparently share this passion that I began years ago, has not left me disappointed right up to this very moment. In fact, the healing, hope, and happiness I feel inside has only grown bigger, brighter, and more powerful. And so have the results – or the rewards of freedom and peace within the entity called "me."

I learned how to make this happen and last with the tools I'm about to give you in the following pages.

Your happiness does not have to come from other people's minds any longer! What others say or do has nothing to do with you. It actually has more to do with them, and how they think, act, believe, and perceive.

Genuinely enjoying your own company is possible, regardless of outside circumstances. Yes, authentic freedom is just around the corner of these pages.

Doesn't that feel great?

I may not be academically approved like Dr. Phil, or a rich and famous Oprah, or possess that "listen to me" media power of Bill O'Reily, but most of us don't. What I do bring to the table is the proof and evidence that anyone who seeks to live in peace, on purpose, and be happy regardless of outside circumstances, can change their life for the better.

These tools can offer you hope and genuine, lasting change. Change to be a happier and healthier person every day of your life, not just when situations seem to be going your way. Believe that you too can be the best person you were created to be.

Perhaps this search for peace and happiness has only been the ghost of a possibility. A feeling in your gut, or an intangible dream, something you could only grasp at but never really hold. You WILL change for the better, I promise, beginning with this very moment, with this very word you are now reading. In fact, it's already begun...

Do you want to be genuinely happy? You can.

You will learn about tools in this book that you may never have known about. I certainly didn't until someone told me. The goal of this book is to guide you to these resources that can give you the lasting happiness you seek. This is why *The Sky is Green and the Grass is Blue* is different from other books. This is a tried, tested, and proven 'walk the talk' guide by yours truly. I am here to tell you that achieving lasting happiness with these methods is an opportunity of transformation you will keep forever.

Isn't that what we all want in life?

To be so happy and peaceful on the inside that it doesn't matter what the heck is going on around the outside. To be free to detach from the negative or often nasty comments people can hit you with unexpectedly. To be able to deal with the inevitable unexpected bombs that crash down in your life, no matter how hard you try to avoid them.

Would you like to repel these negatives in your life, like water that effortlessly rolls off the back of a duck? Unfairness of people, places and things in this world does not have to stop you from living your God-given dream.

This is what you will find in these pages. A stable, consistent set of tools and resources that you can depend on like the impenetrable consistency at the bottom of the ocean to get you where you want to be.

"How could this be a lasting change for me?"

Look at nature. Does the death of winter bring the birth of a new spring? Does the pruned-to-a-nub rose bush come back with more flourishing flowers the following year? Is it possible for a crawling caterpillar, once transformed in its cocoon to become a butterfly, regress back to its original state? No, these changes, which appear to be lasting death, are in fact transformations to a fresher, better life. This is what is going to happen to you.

How would you like to turn everything that you now define in yourself and your life as "upside down" and negative, and transform it into something positive and "right side up?"

How great would it be to know your perceived setbacks are disguised gifts towards the horizon of your greatest comebacks?

It's true!

We will use the tools shared in this book to make the very same pile of manure you hate, into rich fertilizer you love, and regularly utilize it to grow your garden of happiness. Discovering and transforming that "mess" of unhappiness you find so painful to accept, and realizing there is a way for you to change it all into a miracle of personal freedom and lasting happiness, is possible.

Here's an example of trash before, and treasure after, transformational results you can expect to receive after using these new tools.

Before (you have)	Transformed to...	(you get) After
Peace		Anxiety
Confusion		Confidence
Fear		Faith
Doubt		Trust
Resentments		Forgiveness
Selfishness		Purpose
Anger		Acceptance
Pride		Humility
Depression		Joy
Arrogance		Openness
Bitterness		Gratitude
Dishonesty		Integrity
Lies		Truth
Manipulation		Detachment
Despair		Hope
Hatred		Love

The Sky is Green and the Grass is Blue was created for you. Why?

Because I want to give you everything I wish someone else had given me years earlier. How much more time could I have enjoyed? How much more energy could I have directed towards things of purpose and meaning? How much more peacefully could I have lived my life? What else might I have accomplished? What gifts did I never see in my life that could have enhanced my ability to appreciate my life? Yes, this transformation of turning your upside down world right side up will help you be truly happy. This is my purpose, my wish, my prayer, especially for you.

Where ever you go, there you are.

Why not take these positive transformations with you in everyday interactions with your friends, family, co-workers, and relatives. Trust that you're able to transform anything from green sky to blue. And once you are transformed, everything around you is transformed along with you. Don't waste another minute on needless suffering. Take courage, "be steadfast," have hope!

"The diamond cannot be polished without friction, nor man perfected without trials." Confucius

You already own a diamond of happiness, and that would be – YOU!

Happiness is already in there, inside of you, screaming to shine, otherwise you wouldn't be here right now. What you may not believe, what no one has shown you up until now, is how to chip away and remove all that ugly stuff that surrounds your personal diamond of happiness.

The upside down problem that's causing you frustration, misery and keeping you stuck, only exists because no one showed you how to TRANSFORM the mess into a miracle. How to appreciate the very same black junk that's been stubbornly covering up the beauty of the diamond is the very same material that made the diamond so precious in the first place! The pressure of all that unpleasant looking junk around the diamond is precisely what makes it so valuable, so beautiful, and so unique. The same is true for you.

Take comfort, join me on a journey to appreciate, remove, and replace all the black charcoal surrounding the diamond called you, so we can release your own personal dazzling sparkle and shine. Nothing in your life will go to waste.

Even in the midst of a pouring rain storm, you can make a beautiful bright rainbow. Sometimes, the greatest winners in life have lost now and then, causing them to later rise higher, and become a true record breaking champion.

Exercise:

Write down each letter in your first name, and think of something you are grateful for about yourself right now, in this present moment; something about you, something you have, someone you have in your life. It could be any person, place, or thing.

Here is my example:

D Determination to keep a promise.

E Enthusiasm to write this book, and share these tools with you.

B Belief that anything bad can be transformed into something good.

Now, your turn;

_____

_____

_____

_____

_____

CONGRATULATIONS!

Your diamond is starting to sparkle with deluxe dazzle, super sensational, beyond beautiful, fine shine.

People don't change because they see the light, people change because they feel the heat. Pain can motivate you to change for the better. If pain can lead to a good thing, anything can be transformed to bring you a happier good life.

The success of this plan, of course, requires something from you. Yes, indeed, you'll need to bring one piece of "action" into your silent reading of this book on a regular basis. Without it, you can't ever possibly get the happiness you seek, so listen carefully. You are required to bring an active acceptance of this simple statement.

YOU DON'T KNOW, WHAT YOU DON'T KNOW.

You must firmly believe this fact, really believe this statement in the very depth and core of your heart. You will have to accept that out of all the knowledge in the world, this huge planet of data from the beginning of time until this present moment, from every human being that's ever walked the earth, every book that was ever written, every course ever taught, every invention ever created, out of this whole enormous pool of information, you only know a very little itty bitty tiny sliver of it. You may possess merely a speck of this knowledge and truth, an eyedropper full in the mass of an ocean. That's all you know. The simple truth is that you don't know what you don't know. Humbling, isn't it?

Once you accept that you don't know what you don't know, you are open to receive.

The transformation process hinges on this, because it allows you to be open to receiving the gifts along this new journey. Every time you read a thought or a page that brings up your defense mechanism, sarcasm, or cynical inner voice, you need to be actively involved in the process by telling yourself to remove any preconceived notion in your head. Read onward, and repeat these words..."but I don't know, what I don't know."

There's enormous power in that statement, because the words allow fresh space for you to replace the void with the ability to learn, and listen. This is the only way you can possibly ever change. You must first change your thoughts before you can expect to change your behaviors.

Consider that you are not seeing things in your world as they truly are; you are seeing them as you are, through the filter of the interpretation of your personal life experiences in your own mind and emotions. My friend, you must at least consider that your thoughts have been color blind in the past, blocking you from noticing the vibrant colors of truth in the present moment. The sky may have looked green to you, but the true color has always been, and always will be, a beautiful shade of your favorite blue.

Doesn't the idea of having your "thinking vision" corrected feel exciting?

Imagine being your own best friend?

I mean, after all, you do spend more time with yourself than anyone else, don't you? Why not ENJOY your own company? The very fact that you desire to be happy is a sure seal of the promise to receive it.

The only map that can lead you to that place called "happiness," is a willingness to believe it and receive it. You want to go there, to get there, and to live there so desperately you can taste it.

Remember George Bailey in the 1946 movie, *It's A Wonderful Life*? He got what he asked for - relief from all his troubles, "I wish I had never been born."

But the irony of his being able to see what life looked like without him in it was a total disaster! By the end of the movie, he realizes what he thought to be true was completely wrong, and he really did have a Wonderful Life.

Shaking in desperation, he finally begs out loud, through the heavy falling snow battering his broken heart, "Dear God, I want to live again, please Lord, let me live again."

You are going to live again too, fully alive, in your best version possible. You are going to star in your own life's movie with more zeal than you thought possible, imagined, or dreamed. And the academy award goes to YOU, living an authentic, happy, grateful, purposeful life with lasting love.

The following story breathes life into these thoughts. I call it **The Donkey Story.**

"One day a farmer's donkey fell down into a well. The animal cried piteously for hours as the farmer tried to figure out what to do. Finally he decided the animal was old and the well needed to be covered up anyway; it just wasn't worth it to retrieve the donkey. He invited all his neighbors to come over and help him. They all grabbed a shovel and began to shovel dirt into the well. At first, the donkey realized what was happening and cried horribly. Then, to everyone's amazement, he quieted down. A few shovel loads later, the farmer finally looked down the well, and was astonished at what he saw. With every shovel of dirt that hit his back, the donkey did something amazing. He shook it off and took a step up. As the farmer's neighbors continued to shovel dirt on top of the animal, he shook it off and took a step up. Pretty soon, everyone was struck with amazement as the donkey stepped up over the edge of the well and trotted off." Author Unknown

Life is definitely going to shovel dirt on you, all kinds of dirt. The trick to getting out of the well is to shake it off and take a step up. Each of your troubles can be transformed from obstacles into stepping stones. You can get out of the deepest wells solely by not stopping, never giving up! Shake it off and take a step up.

Who doesn't have troubles?

Who doesn't have a skeleton or two in their life history? Who hasn't been hurt, betrayed, or treated unfairly? Who doesn't have a problem they pray would go away? I promise you, everyone has had something they regret having happened to them, or has done something they regret having done to someone else. We all feel pain and sorrow, just like that donkey at the bottom of the pit.

Not everyone has the tools to understand how to take the dirt of disaster thrown on them, and transform it into the stepping stones that can bring us to complete freedom.

The key to the end of the donkey story is that when the donkey released himself from the pit, he ran off, totally free. Had he never entered the pit and overcome his trouble, he would still be tied up and owned by the farmer for the rest of his life. He would have remained a slave to the farmer and never known the difference. His horrible disaster brought him the complete freedom he could never have achieved without it. This is the key: if you have a mess in your life, you have a potential miracle as well.

It only benefits you to keep your mind open at all times.

Your mind is like a parachute - it only works when it's open. Keep your mind and heart open like the parachute, and I promise you'll travel to your new beach home on Peace Island with miles of serenity sand. Wait until you see the spectacular new view from here!

You can't unscramble those scrambled eggs. Why waste a good worry?

There is great power in the now. Give up the hope of a better past, and start focusing your time and energy on a better present moment, right now.

We may not be able to control the direction of the wind, but we can always adjust the direction of our sails. Don't be afraid of change; be very afraid of staying the same.

Exercise:

Imagine you are now on your new home of Serenity Island. Walking on peace beach, you discover Aladdin's Lamp. Curious, you open the cover to find a real life Genie inside. He powerfully emerges out of the lamp growing larger than life, and asks you if you want to be happy? Of course you answer, yes!

He tells you to answer the following questions before your wish can come true.

1. What are you doing when hours pass by like moments?
This is your purpose.

_____

2. When do you feel most at peace and when do you feel most confused?
This is your task to transform.

_____

3. Are you willing to let go of your confusion, replace it with your purpose, and transform yourself to find everything you seek?
This is your happiness.

_____

He tells you, sometimes it is harder to let go than to hold on, and leaves you in a gentle breeze of hope.

Take courage! You're worth the effort!

You are now going to find many treasures and KNOW what you DID NOT know, to be truly happy from the inside out. Existing in a safe place where no one can steal your joy.

Congratulations!

Get ready to celebrate transforming yourself into the unrepeatable, super fabulous diamond of a person, called - YOU.

CHAPTER II

ONE FINGER POINTED AT YOU MEANS THREE FINGERS POINTING BACK AT ME

Have you ever found yourself saying:

- "How could he/she do that to me? Or spontaneously spitting out a long list of justifications for why you were right, and the other person was wrong?
- Repeated the same aggravating thought to yourself again, and again, and again, even when you despised having the thought?
- Frequently find yourself spontaneously defensive when someone criticizes you?
- Get frustrated, angry, or anxious if something is not done perfectly?
- Wait for the other tragic shoe to drop off just around the next corner?

Good News!

If you can admit to seeing yourself in any of the above scenarios, you are already aware that this is a road that leads to no where! You can now choose a different path to help you be happier. By accepting, you've been unknowingly part of upside down thinking, you are now free and empowered to knowingly be part of all the right side up solutions. Doesn't that sound great?

What you don't know is that the very thing that aggravates the living daylights out of you in other people is a gift, a signal for you to know that something inside of YOU is not well.

Once you admit that you didn't know that, you can now begin to identify what that something is, accept it, change it, and let it go. You have to let that destructive thing go, that destructive belief and thinking go, before there can be one inch of room for you to accept the happiness you seek.

Your behavior on the outside is just a mirror in which you show everyone else who YOU most honestly are on the inside. Wow! That's some green sky blue grass thinking to ponder, isn't it?

Let's take an example....

You and your husband, wife, or friend, are enjoying a peaceful evening together. Everything is quiet, nothing much going on. The atmosphere feels quite comfortable and serene.

Suddenly, you start thinking about something this other person did that completely infuriated you. Or you might even be ticked that the person doesn't appear engaged in your presence at all. This fact only adds to growing annoyance.

You begin to think this is just another example of how he/she doesn't care, is apathetic, and how you always have to be the one to do everything all the time. Is your blood boiling?

Suddenly, the words just jump out of your mouth before you can even catch them. "Why did you do such and such the other day," "Why did you not do such and such the other day," or "Why didn't you tell me such and such the other day." You just can fill in the blank with a multitude of "Whys."

The line has been drawn in the sand, and the match to create the bonfire has been lit. Doesn't matter the response, the war has begun. The bombs start flying, pins on grenades removed, perhaps the sound of your voice has gotten louder. One thing is for sure, the river of anxiety under your skin suit is steaming with fumes of blazing hot fire. Yup, that feeling of anxiety, anger, resentment, or betrayal, all those negative emotions you just hate and are all too familiar with, are back again.

But, it's his/her fault. Right?

I'm going to suggest that the argument and the anxiety is just the "flower" at the top of the root of the real problem. We must remove this diseased tree from your garden of your life. It's not the other person who is the real problem, or even your anxiety and/or arguments that go along with them. The problem is inside you. Hence, every time you start to point the finger at someone else, remember there are three more fingers (much more than one), pointing right back at you.

This is good news for you. Why?

Because it means you now realize you have a clear signal and a new stop sign to protect yourself. You now have the ability to pause, and ask yourself the following question: "What's going on inside me right now that is causing this to happen?"

Look, salt only hurts on an open wound, and the very fact that you find yourself upset and in pain, is all the evidence you need to prove that the wound is still open. You need to heal the wound well, so that when salt is thrown on you, you won't feel a bit of pain.

What if I told you that what you feel on the inside will no longer be affected by someone's actions on the outside?

Think of all the energy you can utilize on thinking that is more constructive. You can focus on being in the present moment, when you're not carrying on two conversations in your head. The never ending inner dialogue you have with yourself, and the one you have imagined the other person is having with you. How much happier could you be if all that stressful, internal negative self talk disappeared?

You've been moving in your mind as if you were moving in a rocking chair – you move a lot but you don't get anywhere.

Your losing attempt to achieve happiness is a natural instinct of being excessively familiar with the feeling of unhappiness. Being in the role of victim is a strong subconscious desire leading you to maintain the familiar emotion of victim pain.

My premise is that you are creating your own chaos, because that's simply what you know best. It's as if you want to punish yourself with pain and ridicule. That's all you think you deserve, because that's all the people who surround you have been beating into your ears to hear. You now have permission to, "get off the cross, because we need the wood."

Many thousands of people in this world are afraid to live in a peaceful place because they are afraid of living in any unknown space. This land of undiscovered landscape is a territory called life with no drama. Is there really a life with no chaotic drama to find?

Imagine it is much more frightening for you to feel your deepest feelings, especially the most painful ones, than it is to stand tall in a good fight. So, what do you do? You find a way to create a good fight, a crisis, or any situation that will overshadow the necessity to look inside yourself and feel all those complex emotions.

It is definitely upside down green sky to think this way of avoidance is easier for you. Does an ostrich move to a new location because he buries his head in the sand?

If you grew up with a lot of chaos, that surrounding lifestyle is certainly more familiar to you than the imaginary peace beach you wish you could find.

Let's look at this same scenario another way...

Imagine finding yourself in the exact "my blood is over boiling" scene in this "all about me show" movie. But with these new tools of awareness, you are able to recognize the situation and pause for a moment to conduct a self diagnostic talk with yourself. Perhaps it sounds something like this...

"What is going on inside me right now that I don't want to feel?"

"What events have recently occurred that I don't want to truly face?"

Suddenly you realize that this time last year one of your parents died. That's a traumatic anniversary. Have you talked to anyone about how you feel? Have you talked to yourself about how you feel? Do you feel sad they are gone, or angry that you did not have the closeness and honesty with them you always desired? Do you feel abandoned or let down that life must go on without them? Are you angry with God because they died? Are you regretful of actions or words you never expressed? Do you feel lonely, tired and afraid?

If you haven't asked yourself any of these questions, or if you didn't allow yourself to feel the feelings, they have to escape out of you somehow, somewhere, onto someone.

Like a volcano that explodes under too much pressure, it is impossible to keep toxic emotions inside yourself without consequences.

The upside down factor is this: feeling pain you do not want to feel will give you the opportunity to feel the good feelings you do desire.

You must shout this question out of your mouth loudly for your ears to hear clearly. "My attempt to ignore this pain is creating precisely more of it." Stop!

The root of the issue is simple - you don't want to feel pain.

Consider that you have been well trained throughout your life to do anything to escape feeling pain. You can even create some other type of pain to deal with what appears to be a more controllable situation (in your subconscious opinion anyway), to avoid the true source of pain you experience. You can automatically create acute drama with high shock value. Are you designing a good argument with someone to take that focus away from you?

The relief of being able to transfer all those negative emotions onto another person, place, or thing, has become a priceless bad habit.

Like the passing relief of a quick drug fix, you don't even realize you are digging yourself deeper into the donkey pit.

The actual issue in the story above is the death of your parents. Not what appears to be the immediate problem. The root of the issue is feelings never confronted or embraced relating to the death of your parents. You think the whole problem is the other person's actions in the "now," when it is actually the feelings ignored from the past.

Exercise:

Fill in the following blanks as you feel them to be in this present moment.

I will be happy when I have_____.

If only _____would change, I would be happy.

I will be happy when_____ problem goes away.

If only I had more _____I would be happy.

I will be happy when I accomplish_____.

Do you see that you believe your happiness comes from something outside yourself?

Only when those things are achieved, received, stopped, or started, only then will all your problems in life be solved so you can then finally be happy.

Are the people who have the things you want one hundred percent happy with everything in their life? If THEY are not one hundred percent happy having what YOU think will make you happy, why would you want to believe happiness is anywhere else but inside the diamond of you?

If you are a diamond, it makes sense to keep the focus on yourself, keeping all five fingers pointing on you at all times.

Moving the spotlight onto the precious jewel called you, will bring out all the facets of beautiful colors that vividly shine. You feel happy when you see the rainbow of colors, and know you are even happier to be inside and part of the rainbow itself.

What can you do to kill the disease that robs you of your rightful happiness? How do you inoculate yourself from this destructive infection of the mind?

The first thing you have to do is accept that it will take work and be willing to feel uncomfortable in the beginning. The lie you've been telling yourself, that happiness does not take any effort, isn't any easier or more comfortable, anyway.

You've perpetuated this self defeating lie to convince yourself that keeping everything the same will prevent you from suffering more severely in the future. Or you surrender to this particular suffering because you think there is no other way to change the color of the green sky to blue.

You have decided that you tried it all. Leaving things as they are (that would be you) is somehow less work and pain than implementing the effort to change.

It takes effort to be miserable, and it takes effort to be happy.

Either way, it takes effort. Been there, done that. The only way to get a positive return on your investment (you) is to keep the focus on yourself.

One of the most important tools we'll use to build your life of happiness is the acceptance that you can't change other people.

Bill O'Reilly (www.billoreilly.com) states, "The problem is most Americans do not see people for what they really are – they see them for what they want them to be."

You must make a commitment to seek the truth in yourself and others in order to change and grow into the best version of yourself. You can't change what's possible for you to experience without changing you first.

"But, I'm afraid," you say?

Yes, accepting that people have different values, opinions, and may be living in entirely different realities than you is often scary.

But the only reality you can control is yours.

You can't expect to change other people when you're having a hard time changing just a little bit of you! Only God can change other people. Focus on changing YOU for the happier.

Patricia Evans (www.patriciaevans.com) acknowledges the challenge of facing fear either way, because, "By doing so you may encounter your fear of loss of love of a person. By not doing so, you may encounter your fear of loss of self." You always have a choice.

Sure, it's going to hurt and be uncomfortable and painful to feel your own sadness, think about why you feel guilty, and face your regrets, and fears. No doubt about it. But you're feeling all sorts of crappy feelings when you argue or live in a state of unpleasant anxiety anyway, aren't you?

At least this new travel plan gets you to a destination that's brighter and more peaceful, and the more you practice, the more quickly you'll arrive. About face! Lean into your feelings; don't run away from them.

The other part of the solution demands you ask why it is you always become defensive or engage in arguments so frequently in the first place? Everything seems to be going along so lovely and peaceful, and BAM, someone or something just falls down out of the sky like a bomb, and screws it all up for you. What's up with that?

"I thought I was smart enough to do my homework and avoid this type of tragedy."

Control is an illusion that will keep you isolated in a self-made jail, with endless green clouds surrounding you. They will suffocate you without mercy until death do you part, if you let them.

"How do I transform the green clouds to blue now?"

First, accept this is life. Everyone deals with people, places, and things they don't like or deserve. It's part of being a human being. No matter how much money you have, how beautiful you are, or even how famous, everyone has something that bothers them.

Don't believe me? Just ask around or pick up a tabloid magazine. The facts are obvious. Immediately remove the expectation that someone else is exempt from unpleasantness, sorrow, or pain. It is not true.

Green sky thinking shouts that someone else has the secret.

Secret to what?

A secret that life is easy with a guarantee policy from heaven that you can have a pain free, suffering exempt, and problem free life? That is a powerful green sky lie someone told you to keep you in the green clouds.

Blue sky thinking understands without judgment, that every human being on planet earth who has ever lived or will ever live here in a skin suit, will inevitably face problems, confusion, and fears. Nature itself is a contrast of night and day, winter and summer, life and death.

Every person experiences countless contrasts. "God asks no man whether he will accept life. That is not the choice. You must take it. The only choice is how." Henry Ward Beecher

Second, get rid of the idea that someone else is better than you are, or more important than you. Do you believe because they do this or that, or have this or that, or look like this or that, that they are happier than you are? What will they have one hundred years from now?

We are all human beings on this journey called life, and as Elbert Hubbard said, "Don't take life too seriously; you'll never get out alive."

In the end, we ALL die.

This is a great equalizer. Sometimes you and me, we need to think about death to help motivate ourselves to desire living a better life. Anyone can die, but not everyone can enjoy a life well lived.

Before I sat down to write this book for you, I worked in cardiac surgery medical device sales for about twenty years. Though never a nurse, I did graduate with a biology major. The study of life... HEART surgery...connecting the dots?

One of my favorite previous customers, a cardiothoracic surgeon, Dr. Felix Hernandez, had a great way of bringing this truth into crystal clear view. He powerfully expressed our equal worth as individuals in word and deed. He injected a spirit of humility and humor in his dialogue with colleagues who praised themselves too much. Surgeons who might have believed they were better than everyone else, because they were "prestigious" cardiac surgeons.

Dr. Hernandez would say, "Really, you think so? You think being a cardiac surgeon makes me more important than somebody else? Tell me that at 2:00 am in the morning when your pipes burst in your house, and you need a plumber."

Consider another concept: you have been surrounded by so much chaos in your life, you may have to create it just to feel alive.

You might even think that if you had nothing to complain about in your life, it would be too plain and boring. What would you have to talk about with all your friends?

Everyone you know feels sorry for you because of this issue or that one; what would they think if you didn't have some type of "woe is me" problem to share? You might not even be able to maintain many of your friendships if that's the only subject you ever discuss – your problems and how you've been a victim of some horrible person, place, or thing.

Blue sky thinking means removing the drama.

Let go of the crutches that you think help you move in life easier. Surrender to the knowledge that you are the only person keeping yourself locked up in this misery of unhappiness. You now are learning the skills to transform this upside down world right side up, which will unlock your door to happiness. Please enter; you're invited!

Isn't the time and energy spent on keeping this mirage of safety nets intact a lot of hard work?

Is it worth it? For what purpose?

Is it necessary to hold on to the potential "just in case" excuse to explain to someone else that you didn't cause this or that problem? That it's not YOUR fault? And how has that philosophy been working for you?

How ridiculous the green sky looks here. Blue sky thinking knows that the fear of letting go of all the justifications in life, also takes away the time and energy needed to feed those justifications. These fear based justifications are a miserable infection that prolongs worthless pain.

Be willing to let go of the upside down thinking, and you will have room for the right side up thinking, doing, and being.

Martin Luther King said, "Courage faces fear and thereby masters it." You are in the process of mastering your fears here. Congratulations!

What if you are being abused and someone is truly mistreating you? You might be saying right now, "Well, that's all fine and dandy, Deb, but I just can't just 'think' this abuse away." You're absolutely right. You can't. You do have to go through the process of feeling the feelings, identifying the root or trigger to your negative emotional state and situation, but the fact that the other person may indeed be acting inappropriately is genuine. No, you absolutely should not accept unacceptable behavior.

This leads us back to my earlier premise – ask yourself why you dislike yourself so much that you are willing to allow yourself to be with a person or in a situation that treats you so badly in the first place? Why do you punish yourself like this? Why do you think this is all you deserve?

A teacher in high school sexually abused me. Did I understand what was going on at fourteen? Back in those days, fourteen was more like nine today. No, I did not.

What was I looking for?

I wanted to be loved, just like you, and I was vulnerable and willing to do anything or sacrifice anything to get it. The problem was no one ever showed me or told me lust was not love. Love was not sex.

My color blind green sky thinking thought if I engaged in this "making love" behavior, I would get love made for me automatically. My blue sky thinking has proven to me that love is a verb, an action word, which desires the greatest good for the other, and often proves itself through actions of unselfish sacrifice.

I suspect that perhaps you were somehow, at some point, treated badly in your life as well. Someone in authority sent you the message that you accepted. The lie that you didn't deserve happiness; hence you've gone out of your way to make sure that it's true.

You've been a magnet to a person, place, or thing that absolutely confirms this miserable expectation. Admit that you don't even know how it would feel to be peaceful on the inside all the time. You have never been able to express with conviction, "Wow! I truly enjoy my own company and like myself."

How can you get somewhere you have never been or known about existing?

You can't imagine being there, "happy," because no one has told you or showed you how to make it happen. You think this is all there is to this life, that's this is the best you can do. *As Good As It Gets*, the movie reads.

I'm here to prove to you that you are wrong! I can't get back the time I spent running on the mouse wheel, but the years of joy come back to me in the redemptive knowledge that you will know how to avoid some of the train wrecks that I drove into head first.

Being able to see your own three fingers pointing back at you means you must implement drastic new measures.

You must deliberately place yourself in an environment that helps you keep those three fingers pointing back at you. Successful sabotage which will help you to be happy. Al-Anon teaches keep the focus on you.

This upside down thinking that everything bad happening to you is your entire fault is wrong. Everything good and bad happening to you is bringing you closer to achieving authentic happiness. This can be true for you!

Enlightenment leading to freedom and happiness is an exciting secondary gain of seeing this right side up truth.

Once you begin to see one area of your life that's been affected by distortion, you inevitably begin to notice it everywhere. Similar to when you're looking to buy a new car, maybe a black jeep, you suddenly begin to discover hundreds of black jeeps everywhere. Your radar has picked up the new frequency, and without even trying, your blinded eyes begin to see.

Your reaction to other people, places, and things, serves as a great tool, a mirror, reflecting back the thermometer reading of the temperature inside yourself.

You're just not getting your way, are you?

Fr. Emmerich Vogt, author of the 12-step review (www.12-step-review.org), puts it plainly when he says, "Not getting my way in the past is resentment. Not getting my way in the present is anger. And not getting my way in the future is fear."

Have you ever anticipated feeling resentment, anger, or fear, towards a person, place, or thing? Welcome to the club! False expectations are seeds that can only grow disappointment.

God often places certain people in our lives who may need to overcome similar challenges to our own. We can see the insanity in someone else clearly and immediately, when it is too painful to see the insanity in ourselves.

Once upon a time, a friend of mine always seemed to be going through similar dating experiences as I was. I would start dating a guy who was married twice with children from each marriage; less than two weeks later she would be dating a guy who was married twice with kids. My fairy tale began falling apart from verbal and emotional abuse, and so did hers. She would break up with her guy; I would break up with mine. I would get back with my guy; days later she would get back with hers. The saga went on and on. Same movie, different actors. Always the same destructive, emotional roller coaster with a catastrophic ending.

She could see how sick I was to stay in that insane relationship, the same way I could see it in her, but we could sadly never see it in ourselves.

Years later, and with much effort to correct this color blindness in the mind, we both laugh at ourselves and thank God He gave us our friendship to keep one another on track.

"As iron sharpens iron, so man sharpens his fellow man." Proverbs: 29:17

Sometimes we need to see the pain in others to desire removal of the very same pain within ourselves.

You might think I'm crazy to ask you to invite more pain to get less of it. Without a doubt, this is the most loving gift I could give to you.

The Doctor Story shows you why. Paraphrasing somewhat from a sermon I heard by Fr. Angelus Shaghnessy, OFM, Cap. EWTN (and don't get all defensive because I told you a priest came up with the story, because I can hear you mumbling about it from here!).

"Imagine you have cancer in your breast or prostate, and you come to me as your doctor for help. You tell me you want to live. You want to get well. You want to enjoy the rest of your life. I sit there and tell you I also want you to be happy, as happy as you can possibly be, and enjoy the rest of your life to its fullest. Then I give you the bad news that you have cancer, and send you away out of my office."

"Have I shown you love? Have I helped you get what you want? Have I told you the truth?"

"You're not angry or upset as you leave my office though, are you? Perhaps I didn't tell you anything you didn't want to hear. Has the easy way been the most loving thing I could do for you? No, what I really need to do is tell you that you do have cancer, and the only way for you to get well is to set you up for radical surgery to remove the disease."

"You'll need to realize you will feel more pain, and suffer much more pain than you do right now, in order to be free of the disease and obtain the opportunity to live a happy long life, the real thing you truly want. No, I do have to be honest and tell you it's going to get a lot worse before it's going to get better. The only way to it, is to brace yourself and go through it."

This is the right side up thinking I'm talking about. True blue, crystal-clear, transparent style.

The following is a short listing of a few things that have worked for me, pearls of wisdom discovered through the same abrasive evolution the oyster goes through to transform that gritty dirt into a smooth, iridescent little treasure. I'm sure many others could be added to the list.

Take off your defense armor and repeat after me, "I don't know what I don't know." Some of the happier making tools and transportation vehicles we'll use to build the new happy you are:

- Asking and Listening to God (your higher power of your own faith) - i.e. Prayer
- Any 12 step program
- Individual Therapy and Coaching
- Books, Radio Programs, and CD's
- Inspirational Television and Internet
- Volunteering
- Retreats and Seminars

If you're saying, "I've already been there done that," I would challenge you that there are many specific sources within each of the above mentioned groups that you haven't investigated. I know I hadn't.

And that would be great news for you!

You've done some of the work, gotten some of the help, but all the dots haven't quite connected yet. It's as if you've taken antibiotics before, but sometimes they don't always work well.

The analogy of obtaining proper medication may help clarify the point. If you have a sinus infection and the doctor prescribes you a drug focused towards eliminating a kidney infection, what happens? You might feel somewhat better, but it won't help you with the power and impact or long term result a medication specifically designed just to get rid of a sinus infection would offer you. Do you see what I mean?

"When it gets dark enough, you can see the stars." Charles A. Beard

Be excited you are getting out of the caterpillar suit and into those big bold butterfly wings. The past is over, dwelling on changing that past is like saying, "Please help me saw the saw dust."

Remember, we can't unscramble the scrambled eggs. But we can come up with delightful new recipes to serve and enjoy them.

I'm asking you to jump into the new wings and travel to new happier places – you're worth it. "Deb, did you just say JUMP in?" Yes, exactly.

Joyce Meyer (www.joycemeyer.org) told a great story about observing her granddaughter jump into her arms immediately upon request without the slightest hesitation. She reflected that God wants us as His children to trust like her granddaughter, expressing loving, unconditional confidence that we are safely held in His arms. We should firmly believe, regardless of feelings that He cares for us more than we can understand, or imagine. You are here for a reason.

"God does not throw dice." Albert Einstein

Even the best surgeon in the country can't perform surgery on himself. I know; I've been in surgery more times than I can count.

There is no shame in admitting you need a little help from your friends. You must have the right kind of friends who want the same results.

You need to find people who are passionate to be peaceful, purposeful, and happy, in a solid internal manner; individuals who are willing to give up some good for a bigger great; human beings that are in the process of transforming negative encounters into positive opportunities.

Look for people who are actively demonstrating that they are excited about sharing their time, treasure, and talents, to build a healthy new life for themselves and others. Seek men and women who are not afraid of self critique and self awareness by keeping the focus on them and becoming the best version of themselves.

Understanding that we can not always do for ourselves what we need or want, is in no way being stupid, or incompetent, or a failure. That thought is upside down.

Right side up is being wise enough to accept the situation as it is, and do the next right thing from there. You are now turning your upside down thinking right side up!

Be open minded, because "you don't know what you don't know," and throw away any preconceived notions about the next few chapters.

We are now going to dig into each one of those specific categories mentioned above and examine them in a fresh new way, allowing you to maximize your ability to get healed and happy.

In summary, we are going to find the right antibiotic for your disease, and knock it out of you! Get rid of it!

Do some "divine" surgery!

Then we will keep you on a regular consistent multi-vitamin mind program which you can easily do and take every day. We are going to make sure you're not susceptible to getting sick with the disease called unhappiness ever again.

Be open to these next chapters, not intimidated or insulted. No green sky eyes should be reading these next few pages.

"People seldom improve when they have no model but themselves to copy after." Oliver Goldsmith

Hey, your best thinking kept you stuck in unhappiness; your best thinking isn't going to get you into happiness. You need outside help, to give you fresh new ideas about how to be happy.

We need to use right side up effective tools to build this new right side up happy life. Not with ineffective counterfeit tools, but with long lasting material that can stand up to everyday tsunamis.

"What we learn to do, we learn by doing." Aristotle

This statement still holds true to modern day wisdom. It's time to learn, and start doing, right side up happiness, right now.

CHAPTER III

CONVERSATIONS WITH
YOUR CREATOR - PRAYER

Wouldn't it be great to have a reliable source for the answers you seek every day of your life, anywhere you are, completely free?

Prayer is like that!

Think of Prayer as: **P**eaceful **R**eal **A**nswers **Y**ou **E**njoy **R**egularly.

This is a magical key to turning your upside down world, right side up. It is a self diagnostic system that scans your whole soul for any unhappiness disease, and opens your mind to what, where, and how you can replace the disease with healing, peace, and happiness.

Write it down; make it happen.

Fill in the blanks below with this new knowledge of what Prayer is and how doing it will help you be happy.

P_____R_____A_____Y_____E_____R_____

Let go of, and erase, any preconceived defensive attitude you may have about prayer from this moment forward. Open your mind to the possibility that you may not know all there is to know about prayer.

You can not conceive the unimaginable gifts with your name already on them! There's happiness wrapped up in bright colors with matching bows, patiently searching for your hands to hold, free of charge.

Seeds of prayer will only grow a field of peace, purpose, and happiness.

I often hear friends say, "Well, I've tried everything else; maybe I should try to pray now." Now that's exactly the kind of upside down attitude I'm talking about getting rid of!

Praying should be the very first thing you do – before you attempt to do anything else. Not the last.

Imagine you are sitting in your car wondering why you're not moving yet. "Why is the car I own not moving?" "Does this imperfection in the function of my car have anything to do with me?" You tell yourself, "This problem with my car can't possibly be a consequence of anything I did to it, because I know I am doing everything right."

What is wrong with this picture? You have the key in your hand, but you do not have the key in the ignition. You have not put the key into the ignition, nor have you turned the key inside the ignition forward? How can any system ever turn on without the action of this important step?

A small task in the process of using your car as intended creates a huge successful or unsuccessful result. The desire you seek hinges on your ability to follow the instruction guide given to you by the manufacturer of the car.

The car was designed for a certain purpose, and to work in a certain way. The car functions only in the manner constructed by the inventor. The car comes with a very specific manual to work as promised. It is up to YOU to follow the instruction manual provided to gain access to the benefits of having the car.

Argue with yourself all you want, and continue wishing the car would work differently. Your wishing it so will never make it so. The person who designed that car has the final word. You can futilely disagreeing with this fact, or accept the set of rules already provided to you.

Maybe after much time, frustration, and anger, you eventually give up your hope of the car working another way. You change your thoughts and actions, accepting the reality of the situation.

You now have been frustrated enough to surrender to using the instruction manual to get the car started. Why? Because your desire to move towards your destination is greater than your prideful or perhaps stubborn need to feel you can control changing the way the car works.

After all this chaos and crazy making, you now put your key into the ignition, turn the key, and wow! You see that the car truly does work they way you wanted it to all the time. And it does so, surprisingly, with the least amount of effort on your part.

Now you ask, "Why did I wait so long, and waste so much valuable time not following the free instructions provided?" "I should have just followed the guidelines in the first place." "I would already be where I wanted to go if I just followed those instructions."

You only frustrated yourself and wasted time in disagreeing with, and resisting reading, and following the car usage instruction guide.

Prayer is the key now in your hand. The manufacturer guidelines require you to turn the key forward by praying. This will allow you to travel easily toward the happiness you seek.

Name one thing in this entire world that does not have a specific purpose? I promise you, you can't.

A toaster is designed to toast, a car is designed to take you somewhere, a book is designed to be read, clothes are designed to be worn, televisions are designed to be watched, music is designed to be listened to, and jewelry is designed to be worn. Why would you think this consistent rule of this world is any different for you? Do you think you're designed to just take up space on the earth with no purpose at all?

You are absolutely designed for a specific purpose, to do a specific thing, often many things, in a specific way. You are born; you live; you die.

In the entire world, with all the millions of people that have ever or will ever walk this earth, there is and will be only one, unrepeatable you. What you do between the dash of your life between birth and death is all that really matters.

Dr. Wayne Dyer (www.drwaynedyer.com) in his book, *The Power of Intention*, helps us ask the right question, "How do I find my life's purpose?"

"Suppose, instead, that you know this is a purposeful universe where your thoughts, emotions, and actions are a part of your free will and are also connected to the power of intention. Suppose that your thoughts of being purposeless and aimless are really a part of your purpose. Just as the thought of losing someone you love makes you love them even more, or an illness makes you treasure your health, suppose that it takes the thought of your unimportance to make you realize your value...In a sense, thoughts about your purpose are really your purpose trying to reconnect to you."

I find a lot of comfort in this idea. The fact that you want to know your purpose seals the promises that you will.

Dr. Dyer also wrote an entire book about there being *A Spiritual Solution to Every Problem.* Now isn't that a right side up idea?

How do you know how something works?

You read the directions, right? Who wrote the directions for you? The "entity" that created you, right? God, Higher Power, Universe, call this higher knowledge of unconditional love, whatever you can accept at this moment in time.

No matter how you name this entity, it is imperative you accept this is the only "entity" that decisively knows what you were created to be. You must read this entity's instruction manual to understand how you function properly. This entity invented and created you. This entity gave you a free instruction manual to perform at your optimum happy best.

Prayer is the first key in your instruction manual for you to understand the peace, purpose, and happiness you were designed to offer the world.

"What I see convinces me God exists; what I cannot see confirms it." Albert Einstein

God exists, so get talking in your language of prayer!

Did you ever see the movie, *Saving Private Ryan*? If you did, you may remember that the troops who were on the highest ground had the best tactical advantage against the enemy. The poor suffering soldiers at the bottom, at sea level, were blind and vulnerable to all attacks from their prowling killers. They had no idea who was coming at them. They were blind to when, or where, the enemy could attack.

This vulnerability was not true for comrades sitting up on the mountain high above. These members of the team had a perfect view of everyone below. Friends and enemies alike. How did they help their fellow soldiers in the low sand utilize this useful information? They communicated with each other. They had the proper walkie talkie communication tools to make communication possible with all members of their team simultaneously. Regardless of the location, high ground or low ground, everyone was able to guide each other, through use of these communication tools. This communication was imperative to achieve their ultimate goal of winning the war.

Yes indeed, the soldiers at the bottom ground, who couldn't clearly see anything around them, were now able to utilize the benefits of the information their buddies had from being on the high ground. Based on the information fellow comrades on the high ground gave to those on the low ground, everyone benefited from the few who could see the big picture.

The soldiers at sea level listened, trusted, acted, and followed directions to guide them through the terrain despite the fact they themselves could not see the obstacles. They trusted.

This trust allowed them to succeed. It was much more effective and a whole lot easier for them to navigate the land with this new information supplied by those on higher ground. This communication was the key to helping them avoid the enemy. Could success for them at the bottom have ever have been possible with limited knowledge and blindness at sea level?

Talking to God is just like that scene in *Saving Private Ryan*. God, your Higher Power, is at a strategic advantage to you. God can see the entire timeless picture from the top of the mountain, the top of the universe. He has that tactical superiority of being on the higher ground.

You, on the other hand, can only see what you can see down here at sea level. You don't know what you don't know. You need to communicate with your higher power to get the knowledge, and instructions, to bring you home to safety. This communication tool is prayer.

God, your Higher Power, invented and created you. He wants you to function at maximum happy speed. This is why He placed you into existence.

Does any father or mother not want their child they created to be happy? How could it be any other way with you and your creator?

God desires to tell you whatever you need to know to grow. He desires to assist your winning all wars in this life. He is waiting for you to open your channel of communication. Change the frequency so you can receive His message with clear reception.

Prayer will always give you Peaceful Real Answers You Enjoy Regularly, to learn how to be happy.

Did you happen to see Mel Gibson's movie, *The Passion Of The Christ*?

If you did, I'm sure you remember the ending when Jesus was nailed on the cross suffering his last few suffocating breaths in excruciating pain. Clearly, this could be classified as the lowest of the low points in His life.

The question I believe we need to ask ourselves as we reflect on this scene is what did Christ do during this lowest point of his life? When times were the very worst for Him, what did He do to relieve this pain and suffering?

Did he ask for a few shots of tequila to get drunk and forget about his troubles? Did he ask to see a few good pornography shows to take his mind off the pain? Did he throw a temper tantrum and tell everyone, "See ya', I'm out of here!" Did he revengefully send daggers into the people killing and abandoning him?

No. Jesus did not turn to anything outside himself to find relief during this low point in his life. He turned inward to His Father in prayer. If Jesus turned inward to prayer during this low of all lows in His own life to find relief, I think we too, can try to do the same.

He gave us an example. The things outside ourselves, which may provide temporary relief, are not going to give us permanent relief.

What are those temporary relief fixes we reach for outside ourselves: drugs, alcohol, sex, money, other people, power, or fame. None of these outside tangibles can ever provide healing to an untouchable wound within the heart of any human being.

Our heart bleeds with suffering that we can't put in a box, see, touch, or hold. Yet we know these tragedies of suffering are more real than anything our eyes could ever see, our hands ever feel. Permanent relief within the soul is only possible with a new heart. Prayer is your first transformation tool towards completing your transplant of a happy heart.

Father Corapi (www.ewtn.com), a past multi-millionaire, drug addict, every kind of addict, was a great success by any worldly standard. He had lived in the Hollywood fast lane, with all the rich and famous, for many years. He had everything anyone could ever want.

Suddenly plunged to the depths of despair, living homeless on a park bench in Los Angeles, he now understands counterfeit happiness.

He knows it well, first hand, and it almost killed him. It may be killing you too. Fr Corapi understands and explains the resistance people may have to prayer.

Do you think prayer is somehow beneath you? That it's just a waste of your valuable time? That it is a useless effort with no result? That the coveted intellectual elite may not approve? Do you think prayer requires too much work and effort?

Fr. Corapi asks, "Why do we become slaves in the name of freedom?"

We want genuine happiness and a right side up world, but we continue buying the counterfeit products that never provide it. Isn't that stupid?

Fr. Corapi encourages us to be excited that we ALL have the ability to pray. It is a free gift. It's proof positive that we already have a relationship with God when we pray. We can't even have the desire or willingness to pray if not for God putting it in our hearts in the first place. You can not desire what does not exist. You can't imagine what is not possible for you to achieve.

Prayer, as defined by Webster's dictionary is, "A supplication or expression addressed to God or a god, an earnest request or wish."

You wish you could be happy; you express all your unhappiness to yourself, your friends, and possibly your therapist or coach (for a lot of money).

I am challenging you to express those very same words, desires, and dreams to a specific God, your Higher Power.

How hard is that?

It doesn't cost you any money; you don't have to make a special road trip; it takes virtually no time to do; you can do it anywhere; you don't even need to tell anyone you did it. All you have to do is say the very same thing you've been saying and asking yourself and everyone else around you, except this time you have to intentionally direct those words to God.

Now, you may hear that little voice inside your head arguing, the self critic yelling, "I'm not going to do that; I don't even believe there is a God." Or you might say to yourself, "I've already tried that and nothing happened."

Recall the law of no/know: You don't know what you don't know, and do it anyway.

Could it be arrogance or pride inside your head that obstructs your ability to consider something exists that knows more than you

(God)? Is it your fear of rejection that blocks you from imagining that an all knowing God could think you were precious enough just as you are that he would enjoy listening to you? Are you perhaps afraid you'll actually get what you ask for?

It takes humility to put prayer into action because, in order to pray, you must admit the following:

1. You don't have all the answers.
2. You need help from something outside yourself to get where you want to be.
3. You are loved by something/someone that will actually take the time and enjoy listening to whatever you're saying, no matter what you are saying.

What do you do with your friends when you get together for dinner? Do you sit around, eat, and just look at each other at the dinner table?

When you're at work, do you walk into your office or a meeting, sit around the conference table and smile at each other, leave, and think to yourself, "Wow! What a productive meeting that was; we accomplished a ton of great stuff!"

When you get married, do you look at your future husband/wife, smile through the whole ceremony, hold hands, and walk away to live happily ever after as husband and wife without future words? Of course not!

There is no way you can communicate or function in getting to know or enjoy another person unless you open your mouth and say something to them, and open your ears to hear them. Similarly, there is no way you can get to know or enjoy the rewards of knowing your God if you never talk with Him by praying. It's that simple.

How many times have you been at the beach, observing some stranger painfully attempt to precisely tune his/her radio station (non digital of course – baby boomers will understand this scene much better), to a specific channel? They tirelessly attempt to remove any annoying static that could be chopping up the clarity of their song.

Why do they do that?

They do that because it is important for them to thoroughly enjoy the pleasure of listening to their favorite music. The effort and work they must endure is worth the final pleasure of enjoying static free music.

It is impossible to remove the static without finely tuning into the station. Perhaps this task is not always easy to achieve, or quick to accomplish. But they find the enjoyment of listening to their favorite song absolutely worth the time and effort.

I promise you, if you put in one half that amount of effort into removing the static in your surroundings, the chaos that clutters your mind, you will most assuredly be able to hear the inspirational song God has written just for you. Aren't you worth the effort?

Here are some examples of how I put prayer into action in my everyday life;

I get up in the morning, brush my teeth and say, "Thank you God for everything." That is a powerful prayer. I pour my morning coffee and say, "Please help me God to make a positive difference today with all the people I meet." I put my coffee cup in the dishwasher and say, "God, I'm inviting you into my day from beginning to end, protect me and guide me." I go upstairs to get dressed and say, "God, please protect and guide my loved ones today." I always ask to do His will, not mine, because I know from experience, His plans for me are significantly better than my own.

Painless, quick, easy, and free. It's certainly a catalyst for a healthier "gratitude attitude" to fuel my entire day.

Exercise:

Name three short thank you prayers you can say to God tomorrow morning as soon as you wake up.

1._____

2._____

3._____

Tony Robbins (www.tonyrobbins.com) talks a lot about the power of gratitude prayer first thing in the morning in his bestselling program, *The Edge*.

He explains it is imperative for you to deliberately tell yourself and God what you are grateful for in your life each day. "I want to believe you exist God; show me if you do. Help me God. I pray that whatever is interfering with my Higher Power's will for me may be removed."

These are all prayers. It does not matter what you say, how you say it, when, or where you say it.

What matters is that you say it – something – to your God.

If you want to know someone, you talk to them. If you want to know God exists and He cares for you and can change your life for the better, you have to TALK to Him, too.

The more you do it, the more you'll enjoy it, the better you'll feel, the more positive change you'll see in your life, and the more you'll be asking yourself why it took you so long to enjoy prayer in the first place!

Deepak Chopra's (www.chopra.com) often speaks and writes about the power of meditation.

Is it any coincidence that meditation rhymes so well with medication? I don't think so! Meditation is a medication for your mind, body, and soul.

The ancient monks knew this when they meditated on the life of Christ through the Gospel Prayer of the Rosary.

Did you think all those Catholics were walking around with voodoo beads? No, they were meditating on the life of Christ with, and through the eyes of His mother, Mary, the mother who knew Him best, the mother who was closer to Him than any other person in His life. She was with Him from birth until death, throughout his entire life.

Through her eyes, we come to think about the things that Jesus did when He walked the earth. The person praying is so deep into this meditation of the life events of Christ, they can lose all track of time. The touch of the beads helps the person keep moving into the next joyful, luminous, sorrowful, or glorious mystery of the prayer. The physical, mental, and spiritual senses are engaged in union simultaneously through the rosary prayer.

We magnify what we focus on, and I can't imagine anything but good resulting from magnifying healing and holy people, places, and things. Is it any surprise that part of the word holy is inside the word wholeness?

You may be asking, "How does this prayer thing work, anyway?"

Or you want to understand all the elements that prove it definitely works before you even begin. You might have a scientific mind that requires a technical, prospective, randomized study on the effectiveness of prayer before participating in the action.

Answer the following questions and you will have your answer to the above questions.

Do you understand how your television set works? Can you take it apart and put it back together again? Can you explain one theory behind why a plane can get off the ground? How does your internet system work? Can you build the computer that works in conjunction with it?

You probably answered no to all of the above questions. However, you probably do not boycott using your TV because you don't understand how to build one. You have not stopped getting on planes for vacation because you don't understand the theory of how the plane fly's. And, I am sure you do not deny yourself use of your computer and the internet because you don't understand how either one works well enough to build the system on your own.

Do you not see what a hypocritical double standard you have with God, with prayer?

You do not have to understand everything under the sun to enjoy the benefits it offers.

You do not have to understand God or prayer to be able to enjoy the happiness they bring. Which is more important to you? Having to understand, or wanting to do whatever it takes to be happy?

The following story vividly expresses the essence of prayer. It did for me at least, when I first heard it. I pray it has the same positive effect for you. I call it **The ABC Story**.

"While walking through the woods one day, I was surprised to hear a child's voice. I followed the sound, trying in vain to understand the child's words. When I spotted a boy perched on a rock, I realized why his words had made no sense; he was repeating the alphabet. "Why are you saying your ABC's so many times?" I asked him."

"The child replied, "I'm saying my prayers.""

"I couldn't help but laugh. "Prayers? All I hear is the alphabet.""

"Patiently the child explained, "Well, I don't know all the words, so I give God the letters. God knows what I'm trying to say.""
Author Unknown

It's not what you say to God that matters, what matters is that you say it with a sincere heart. The spirit of your soul brings meaning to the message, and the very fact that you try to pray at all, is the only prayer you'll ever need, anyway.

You learn to love by loving; you learn to pray by praying.

George Jean Nathan shares, "No man can think clearly when his fists are clenched." When you pray, you must unclench your fists. Only then, can you think more clearly and see happiness.

Incorporating the discipline of prayer in your new tool box inevitably leads to your happiness. Upside down thinking believes self discipline is self destruction. Right side up thinking knows self discipline is self preservation.

Marcus Grodi (www.chnetwork.com) gives a great example of self discipline leading to happiness using an analogy with trains. I call this **The Train Story**.

"What do trains do? Trains take us places. Where do you want to go? To the land of perpetual peace, purpose, and happiness. How will the train get us there? Will it follow a path, a map, a predetermined course? Yes, it will. And what will be the primary component the train must have available to make that happen? Have you guessed yet? Railroad tracks."

"When you get in a train and it runs super fast, and stays within the tracks do you say to yourself, "I feel suffocated, constrained, like a hostage moving within these very narrow tracks." No, you feel safer when the train stays on the tracks because you know those tracks keep you on track!"

Prayer is like that. Prayer is like a train track allowing you to arrive at happiness safer and faster. Yes! Another green sky moment turned blue! Woohoo!

Two thoughts can't occupy the same space at the same time. Shovel out that negative thinking by injecting positive prayer into your mind. You will be much happier and a whole lot more peaceful.

"If you change your thoughts, you change your world," Dr. Norman Vincent Peale

No God – No Peace; Know God – Know Peace.

St. Francis DeSales often said, "Half an hour's meditation is essential except when you are very busy. Then a full hour is most definitely needed."

Exercise:

Using your last name, write down a prayer which will benefit yourself, someone you love, or a problem you want to be solved for a person or a group who suffers in our world. What do you want for yourself or them? Turn that into your prayer.

Here's an example using my last name, SCOTT.

S   Show me God, who you want me to pray for today.

C   Charity. I pray that all people everywhere will have charity, love, and compassion for other people who suffer the loss of their loved ones.

O   Open my heart to be a better discerning person. May my encounter with everyone I meet leave them being a better person, a happier person, a smiling person.

T Terrific teens. I pray for young people everywhere to be protected and have the strength and courage to be the best they can be according to Gods will for them.

T Trust. To trust you God, in your tender loving care for me, especially when I feel alone, abandoned, helpless, and do not understand.

Now, your turn;

Last Name _____
Use first letter of last name to begin the prayer.

_____

_____

_____

_____

_____

_____

Congratulations!

You are radiating the brilliance of that one-of-kind, intricately faceted, sparkling of a diamond jewel called - you.

In closing this chapter, let me share my prayer I say for YOU.

"Do not look forward to the changes and chances of this life in fear; rather look to them with full hope that as they arise, God, whose you are, will deliver you out of them. He has kept you until now; do but hold fast to His dear hand and He will lead you safely

through all things; and where you can not walk, He will bear you in His arms. Do not look forward to what will happen tomorrow. The same everlasting Father who cares for you today will take care of you tomorrow and every day. Either he will shield you from suffering, or He will give you unfailing strength to bear it. Be at peace then, and put aside all anxious thoughts and imaginations."
St. Francis DeSales

Chapter IV

Don't Go It Alone - Programs

What is a program?

Webster's defines a program as, "A brief outline of the order to be pursued or the subjects included (as in a public entertainment); a plan of procedure; coded instructions."

Your program is going to help you achieve the happy order you desire to pursue and receive. You'll be the smiling and happy diamond star, shining in the spotlight. Doesn't that sound like something you want to experience?

Your program will:

- Give you a clear, easy to follow map to Happiness Island.
- Provide a consistent reference guide to unlock all your hidden treasures on Happiness Island.
- Offer instructions on how to walk on Happiness Island's peace beach everyday.

Dr. Michael Murdock says, "If you want to get something you've never gotten, you've got to do something you've never done."

What if I told you this happiness program is completely free? How would you like that? What if I also told you, it never costs more than a mere one dollar donation? Would that be an affordable price, in exchange for feeling happy on a regular basis? Good news; it is now available in towns near you!

What is the name of this program?

Please stop for a moment and collect your law of no thinking. You don't know what you don't know. Ready? Excited? Here it is!

The name of this is gift is...drum roll please...a simple twelve step program. Yes! Twelve stairs to heaven; twelve simple ways to live a happy life all the time; twelve basic rules to follow which keep your train on the tracks. All of these are easy to achieve, regardless and despite the external circumstances that may surround you.

A great tragedy you may falsely believe is that twelve step programs are just for really sick people. Or that a twelve step program is certainly not for you.

Typically, people associate Alcoholics Anonymous with all twelve step programs. I know I did. But what you don't know is that almost anyone can benefit from a twelve step program. There are more of these programs devoted to a multitude of problems than you probably ever imagined.

"How can a twelve step program help me turn my upside down world right side up, and which one would help me the most?"

These are important questions to answer. The most important action you can implement this moment, is to say a prayer which asks your God to help you maintain an open mind. Ask for a willingness to consider how a twelve step program might help you get all the happiness you've ever been seeking.

Participation in any twelve step program demands that you keep the focus on yourself. Twelve step programs offer you a safe and compassionate place to go, where you can keep those three fingers looking back at you.

The benefit of being a part of any twelve step program is that it ensures you will be at least "trying" to focus on a God/Higher Power, rather than you, and your problem.

As Joel Osteen (www.joelosteen.com) likes to say, "It's amazing how the bigger we make our God, the smaller all our problems become."

Another gift offered through participation in this program is that you at least have a program to begin with. How many times do you say to yourself, "I don't have a choice in this matter, decision, or situation?" Such thinking creates anxiety, frustration, fear, and a fair amount of emotional claustrophobia.

Negative feelings, and thoughts, can only create more negative thoughts and actions. None of that is good. Being part of a twelve step program means you are in a program. You may not do it perfectly, but at least you have it.

"The journey of a thousand miles begins with a single step." Lao Tzu

Years ago, when my therapist suggested I go to Al-Anon, it took many months before I was willing to try it. My response was perhaps similar to yours, "That's just for crazy, sick people." How wrong I was.

I vehemently resisted the possibility that I was qualified to be a member of a twelve step program, and certainly did not think it could ever help me. I was wrong.

I was completely upside down in this thinking. So deeply entrenched in green clouds, I now share that my joining a twelve step program was, and is, the single most effective activity that I have done to help me change for the better.

A one dollar donation, that's all it takes, to give me a million dollar reward. The upside down irony of the least expensive program providing the most priceless reward towards happiness is a secret no longer.

Picture this gal walking into a meeting. Alone, afraid, crying, desperate. She has no hope left in her soul. Her fiancée is gone, her job perhaps in jeopardy, she can't concentrate on the slightest task. She feels tired, exhausted, confused. She can't hold a steady conversation, and she can't look anyone in the eye without the escape of a tear. She is riddled with shame, and emotionally paralyzed. She hates herself for what she has, and has not done. She considers there is no purpose to existing anymore, and decides God does not exist either.

It took this depth of pain to drag her into the walls of Al-Anon. The internal bruising hemorrhaged blood relentlessly. Her soul felt empty as a black hole. Embarrassed and sobbing, she crawls to find a seat in the back of the room with nameless strange faces.

She doesn't know herself. She asks herself why she is even alive. What hope could that poor girl ever have of a productive future? What could she ever give to the world that could be of any good to anyone? Do you think she is a failure? Do you think the possibilities for a happier future exist for her? Do you think her story will finish on this miserable low?

What if I told you that I was that tragic gal? It's true. Never give up hope on yourself. Never give up the hope that God can and will bring a greater good out of a terrific bad.

Never give up. Never!

A friend of mine waited four years, not four days or months, I'm talking about four YEARS; before she finally attended an Al-Anon meeting once it was suggested to her. I told her it had helped me to change, and I was confident it would help to change her for the better too.

She asked for my advice, and enjoyed the answers I provided, but resisted going to the source of those answers in Al-Anon.

On the outside, this dear friend was intelligent, kind, beautiful, and successful by any worldly definition. A most loving person, the most dedicated friend one could ever hope to have.

The problem was, her inside did not match her outside. She lived in a perpetual state of conflict with many friends and family. Not a day seemed to go by without some form of catastrophic problem or disaster.

Suddenly, after four years of consistent invitations, she called me in a deeply distressed voice. After a long pause, she stated simply, "I want to go to one of those Al-Anon meetings this Thursday. Will you go with me?" Wow! Out of what appeared to be no where, she was finally ready to unwrap this gift delivered to her door. I couldn't have been happier for her.

The result? After attending her first meeting, my friend turned to me with a short, "Thank You." This wasn't just any casual thank you; this comment contained pure avalanche power.

Don't wait four years, months, or days. Do it now. Don't waste one more second resisting. Get yourself involved in some type of twelve step program immediately. A program that will help you get your heart and mind healthy in ways you can not now even imagine. I am your living proof; a twelve step program can change your whole life for the happier.

Do not be stubborn, cynical, or afraid.

Try it, and if you don't like it, you have lost nothing but an hour of your time, and potentially gained a lifetime of everything you ever wanted. A one dollar investment in you can yield a million dollar spiritual return. How great is that?

"How will attending this program change me for the happier?"

Is forgiveness a feeling, or an action?

Many people find it impossible to forgive, because they believe forgiveness is in the feeling. Feelings aren't facts. Forgiveness is in the will. If you do not wish or try to return evil to the person who has harmed you, if you pray for them, if you don't gossip about them, if your actions wish them the best to be a better person, even if you feel emotionally that you can't stand them, you have still forgiven them.

Many of your perceived definitions may be upside down. You can not be happy until you are able to turn this right side up. A twelve step program is a transformation machine for green sky to blue.

You need to stop drinking arsenic and expecting the other person to die.

These programs help you begin by forgiving yourself first. You keep the focus on yourself, to make yourself the better person. You're the only person you can control anyway. Walking up and down these twelve stairs will be healthy exercise to clear your mind of upside down thinking disease.

One of my favorite Al-Anon sayings is, "Take what you like, and leave the rest."

What a great way to live your whole life. There will always be people, and things in your life you don't like. You will not always like or agree with everyone you meet. Despite this fact, you can always find something positive in every situation, a pearl of wisdom, to help you become someone wiser. Knowledge is power for a happy life. Remember, every pile of manure can be transformed into your highest quality fertilizer, given the proper environment.

When you join a twelve step program, you are bringing your perceived bad life events, into antibiotic walls. These walls contain the tools to transform the upside down into the right side up.

Don't you want to get some value out of all that pain and suffering and unhappiness you've been going through? Don't you want to release the diamond out of the black coal? I challenge you to believe that the bigger your mess, the greater your potential miracle.

Twelve step programs are about recovery.

Webster's dictionary defines the word recovery as, "to get back again, to regain normal health, poise or status; to make up for; to reclaim."

What are you reclaiming and getting back?

The person you were created to be. Deep inside, when you were born, before all the experiences of your life changed you into the person you are today, you were designed for a specific purpose to do a specific thing.

What you need to recover are those life giving attributes that were stolen from you. The bad events that caused you pain, stole your clear blue thinking. These events distorted your positive thinking away from the truth, and toward the negative lies.

Those very things you hate and wish you never experienced, given the right environment (a twelve step program), can be transformed into the very things that you love and appreciate the most, awareness that helps you achieve what you most desire. You could never be the diamond you are without the pressure you experienced!

You have a choice: you can live the rest of your life being bitter about all that manure in your life, or you can become better by turning that manure into rich, useful fertilizer. Bitter or better; hostage or happy; miserable or magnificent; it's all up to you.

This analogy is one you may enjoy. I call this **The Card Playing Story.**

"When you sit down to play a card game, any game, pick one you like, you get dealt a hand of cards. You have absolutely no control of what cards you are dealt, and neither does anyone else playing the game with you. Everyone is on equal ground."

"At some point, everyone turns over their cards to see what they were given. Here is where the game truly begins, the point that separates the skilled and the experienced, from the amateur and beginner."

"Everyone thinks, "How can I win the game with the cards I have been dealt?" One person may have a very bad hand, but potentially wins the game because he/she knew how to play with success, maximizing the benefits of the cards given them. Someone else may have a winning hand, but because he/she gave up to a bluff, they lost the game."

"At first glance, the winner should have been the looser, and the looser should have been the winner. The person with the best hand of cards lost the game they should have easily won." Author Unknown

In life you are dealt a set of cards; some good, some bad, good experiences, and some bad ones too. Everyone must do the very best with the cards they are given in this game called life.

The difference between the happy and miserable is in what people do with the life experiences given them. Learning how to maximize good cards, and minimizing the effects of bad cards, is a key to happiness.

The card playing expertise of the self assured poker face, expressing what may or may not be true, boils down to having a certain attitude and confidence. It takes a heck of lot of experience to be good at it. Solid tools for this type of disease will give you clear discernment to distinguish the difference between the truth and the lies.

Participating in a twelve step program gives you an opportunity to learn and succeed through the experience, hope, and knowledge of other people who hold similar cards as you. People who learn how to transform a bad life experience and successfully be happy, win. Those people who share their knowledge of transforming bad into good, shortens your learning curve to accomplish the same success. You won't know what a winning hand you have until someone teaches you how to play like a winner.

Exercise:

Name three bad cards you feel you have been dealt in life that you want to get rid of.

I want to get rid of
Having_____.

I want to stop
Doing_____.

I want to end
Feeling_____.

Now name three good cards you want in replacement for the bad one.

1. I want to Have_____

2. I want to start
    Doing_____.

3. I want to start
    Feeling_____

Congratulations! If you can write it down, you can make it happen.

One of the most debilitating places to be, one of the most paralyzing in my experience, has been the false belief that you don't have any choice. That feeling of being a victim and prisoner is a poison in your mind and not true! We always have choices.

Recovery work, attending a twelve step group, opens your mind to the multitude of choices other people have tried: fresh new ideas to help overcome obstacles into stepping stones, setbacks to comebacks, green sky to blue. These people, who may battle the same or similar situations to yours, give you free wisdom and solutions they have experienced. Some have worked better than others have.

It is amazing how the mere action of being willing to listen, can ignite such radical change in conscious and subconscious beliefs.

You must first change a thought before you can hope to change a behavior. Listen without judgment.

Are you perhaps telling yourself, "Someday I'll try that?" This thinking is not going to get you anywhere. You have to call one of the numbers listed in this chapter, go search the website, find out where a meeting is being held, and go. You have to go to get. If I can crawl into those four walls, battered and broken beyond recognition, anyone can.

Joyce Meyer (www.joycemeyer.org) said something great about needing to get off your tail and just do it, regardless if you feel like doing it or not. "You don't get up in the morning and expect your clothes to jump off the rack onto your body, do you? Why do you expect anything else in your life to just happen for you like that?"

You have to go through the process of taking the clothes off the rack and putting them on, to be able to wear them. You have to go to a twelve step meeting to wear the benefits and achieve the results that go along with it, too.

Simple. Simple. Simple.

I had an English teacher in high school who said something once that I still think of often. We asked why we had to go through all this energy to remember the dates and names of all these famous writers, all dead, when we would probably never be asked about a single one of them, ever again, for the rest of our lives. We told him this effort seemed like a worthless waste of time.

Dr. Garth Pitman, standing confidently in front of our class, responded easily and boldly to our question. In his distinguished, debonair style, he surprisingly agreed. What a shock! After a long pause, and with the strongest conviction, he declared, "It's my job to help you think more critically, to increase your ability to think well. The more you are forced to study and memorize, the larger the memory net in your mind becomes. The larger the net, the more it grows, the more you can learn. I'm here to help you increase the size of your net so you can easily catch more knowledge." It wasn't about the dates of the kings and queens, it was about the process of having to memorize that was important.

Going to twelve step programs increases the size of your net, so you can catch more happiness in your everyday life. It gives you a light within yourself that is uniquely yours, light that illuminates your way, wherever you go.

"If a man carries his own lantern, he need not fear the darkness." A lovely Hasidic saying.

Don't focus on not being able to see too far off in the distance.

No one knows the future in a blue sky world. You don't worry about driving your car through the darkest night because you have headlights to show you the road. The headlights on your car only allow you to see a few feet in front of you. Do you worry you will not get to your final destination if you can not see it within the short view of your headlights? No, you trust the process. You know from experience, little by little, hour by hour, that you will arrive at your destination if you follow the road you can see, and keep going.

Your life is often like those headlights. You can only see a small fraction of what is right in front of you. Focus on the next right thing, the next good step, and the next road you can clearly see.

If you carry your own tools, you don't have to borrow someone else's. Doesn't the thought of total freedom make you feel absolutely great? You don't ever have to be afraid of the dark if you carry your own internal light.

Sometimes, I think because bad things do happen to good people, we tend to throw away the whole notion that we could really find any good in these bad things at all. Remember, those bad times along the way are not the end of the story. You are not finished yet! It's not over, until it's over. If you're reading this, you're not dead yet. Life is not over for you, so keep hope alive!

When I was in cardiac surgery sales, the operating room director of Massachusetts General Hospital taught me a life lesson I will never forget. In the midst of converting product, I encountered a hostile department director who treated me with nasty outrage. She did not want me to take my competitors' product out of her operating room suite. Feeling horrible, despite the fact that I possessed all the appropriate approvals to implement the conversion, I went to tell Bob McDonough, the director, what happened. I anticipated a real scolding for this one!

Unfazed, Bob looked at me and said, "Deb, how many surgeons and directors, and nurses, and multi level personnel do you think I deal with in a day?" Big pause.

I whispered, "Hundreds?"

"Yes, that's right. And I have to get the job done for the best interest of this hospital, knowing there will always probably be twenty-five percent of the people who will disagree with my decisions. If I spent my day focusing on the twenty-five percent that disliked me instead of the seventy-five percent of people who liked what I was accomplishing to make Mass General better, I would never accomplish anything. Focus on the seventy-five percent and forget about the twenty-five percent."

Bob McDonough taught me a lesson I've never forgotten. It is a lesson you have now learned, too. If you want to do something worthwhile with your life, focus on the good, the positive, the seventy-five percent. Gracefully accept that there will always be the other twenty-five percent who may not like you, or what you are doing. Do it anyway.

Be one of the seventy-five percent, and give a twelve step program a chance to give you happiness. Be open to the opportunity. Allow the program to provide you with the tools to find that treasure in the donkey's pit. Transform the caterpillar into the butterfly. Turn your upside down world right side up.

Focusing on twenty-five percent of the picture is upside down. It is not the whole truth. You must turn your eyes to the other seventy-five percent to see the whole picture right side up. If you have been obsessed with the negative twenty-five percent, you will never know the positive seventy-five percent even exists. You don't know what you don't know.

Have you ever heard the story about, **The Tapestry Of Life**?

"Needlework on the top of the tapestry is a colorful symphony of pleasure to the eyes, patterns that easily fit and flow. The tapestry underneath is exactly the opposite. It is knotted and rough. Do you focus on the top of the tapestry, or the bottom? Do you resent the ugly knots underneath, or accept they must exist to create the beauty above?" Anonymous

"All things work together for good." The Bible

You might be thinking, "The God who wanted us to hear that one is surely a liar! Make that statement to a person who lost a loved one on 9/11, a loved one in Iraq, a child that was killed by a drunk driver, or a woman beaten to a pulp by a husband who still says he loves her."

I can hear the voice of Annie, my hairdresser, responding with such conviction when we discussed this very thought. She had been diagnosed with breast cancer at the young age of thirty-four. At the time, she was married and pregnant with her second child. A small lump in her breast and a biopsy validated the cancer, and within weeks, she not only had one breast removed, but the other also, along with having to unwillingly abort her baby because of the devastating chemo treatments.

Here was a lady who could have been bitter, and boycotted God with a lot of apparently good reason. Ironically, her response was unwavering. "Why do bad things happen to good people? Would you pay attention, would you be motivated to change, if they happened to a mean jerk that deserved it? No, you'd say they got what they should have, and move on. But when something bad happens to someone who is good, and doesn't seem to deserve it, you stop and pay attention to what they are doing and say in response to the bad thing that's happened to them. This is why they can make a difference."

The following excerpt is taken from one of those $1.00, 3" x 5", throw it in your handbag for when you have some free time, booklets. I think it provides a fresh take to an old question many of us have asked about how all these bad things can add up to anything good for us. I call this **The Angel Food Cake Story**.

"All things work together." Not separately or independently, not each thing in itself, but "together." God does not promise all things work for good, or each thing is good in itself, but "all things work together for good." Many people pick out one experience in life and wave it in the face of God and challenge, "I don't see any good in that." No, and God doesn't say there is, but it is a part of the "all things," a part of the divine pattern. The separate events of life may seem to be disastrous, but "together" they "work for good." It takes a blending of the experiences in life to make the "together." When we live in submission and obedience to His will, every event has a definite place in the plan and pattern of God. Each thing is a part of the "all things" and "all things together work for good." Sugar is sweet to the taste and adds flavor to much of our food. However, you would not want to make a meal of sugar alone. Nothing would be more sickening. Neither would you want to eat dry, tasteless flour, nor can I imagine anything more nauseating and tasteless than attempting to eat raw egg whites. However, these three ingredients, as tasteless and unpalatable as they are by themselves, mixed together by the hands of a skillful cook, make angel food cake." J.C. Brumfield, *Comfort for Troubled Christians*

Consider participation in a twelve step program as being your oven to make your very own Angel Food Cake, the winning environment, to turn all those sweet and sour thoughts in your mind, right side up. Transform all the experiences in your life into something good.

Take a moment to think about what "good" genuinely means. Is good a feeling of being warm and fuzzy? Is good a reward of financial freedom? Is good the promise that you will never have another problem in your life? What exactly is good?

By definition, Webster's describes good in the adjective form as, "of a favorable character or tendency; bountiful." As a noun it is, "something good; benefit, welfare (for the good of mankind)." In other words, something good is not about a feeling, it is about an overall result being a benefit to something larger.

Be aware that your feelings are not facts.

I know for myself, I lived my life on automatic pilot. If I felt sad and depressed, my life was sad and depressed. If I felt unloved and unappreciated, everything screamed like a neon sign, "You are unloved and unappreciated." If I felt a certain way, good or bad, that was the truth and reality my mind believed as well. My feelings ran what I did or did not do, because my thinking and mind believed everything my feelings said.

No wonder I never felt like life offered me any choices! Maybe you feel the same way now. I was a victim to my own emotional bad weather conditions. The truth is, emotions just let us feel what we are currently thinking at any given moment in time. Nothing more, nothing less.

Feelings exist for a reason. Like a red stop sign in the road, or a green traffic light, they can help us discern better choices. Prompting us to stop and think about what, and why we are having this feeling. We are then freely empowered to make a right side up choice. How great is that?

A twelve step program will give you a vehicle to rise above your feelings and look down on a situation from a more balanced perspective. It will help you understand what it is you feel. Give you new insight and awareness to change your upside down thinking. This awareness of green clouds engulfing you will give you the ability to transform how you think and act.

You will come to realize you are not alone, and that one change can help relieve the burden of stress that keeps you stuck in the upside down rut.

Imagine you are down on the ground, in the pouring rain. You look up to the sky and can only see vast levels of rain filled clouds. From where you stand, you can't see anything above the clouds. But you are aware of a vehicle called a plane. You know if you can get on a plane, the plane will take you above the clouds. You know without seeing it, that there is sunshine above the clouds radiating healing rays of warmth, even in this very moment you stand drenched in the rain.

You are not insulted, or resistant, to engage the help of a vehicle to get you above the clouds, to some sunny location you want to be. You get on the plane, rise above the clouds, and see the sun shinning for miles of smiles. You now are able to look down on those clouds and see them in a completely new perspective. They move in the wind, without substance or strength.

You notice the clouds don't seem to be moving, but know that you are. You are in the steady, silent arena of looking down on the entire collection of clouds. Clouds that no longer are able to effect your surrounding weather conditions, clouds that have no effect on you, in any way, any longer.

You rise above your thoughts in the same way. Your thoughts are like all those clouds. When you get above your thoughts, you are in a completely different position of power and strength to change your direction, actions, thoughts, and feelings.

"If we do not change our direction, we are likely to end up where we are headed." Ancient Chinese Proverb

How else are those clouds like your feelings?

Let's say the sunshine represents a fact. Your feelings are the clouds. You might be all afraid and depressed, thinking the worst in a situation. No matter what anyone tells you, you're in a cloud of doom and gloom. You look up at the sky, and all you can see are gray and black clouds. All you can feel is the rain pouring down around you.

Despite how you feel, you know from experience that there is a different weather condition out there in another location. You are positive the sun is most definitely shinning somewhere.

Based on this factual knowledge (the sunshine), despite how you feel (the clouds), you are smart enough to get yourself on a plane (a twelve step meeting) to go to that somewhere else that you know for sure is sunny.

Once you are above the clouds of feelings, the fact of the sunshine is within clear vision. Now, you can look down on your feelings, those ugly gray clouds, and see them for what they truly are, empty, without substance, weak ghosts. You suddenly realize you were crazy to give away all your power to such a fake, false entity. Why did you ever waste your time believing the lie?

The sun is always shining above the clouds. Your mind is always able to find, see, and enjoy the good that comes out of any life situation. Be willing to get above your feelings with a little help from your twelve step friends.

Fr. Emmerich Vogt of the 12-step-review (www.12-step-review. org) talks about how we can get so wrapped up in other people's lives, we might think, when we die, "we'll see someone else's life flash before our eyes."

Keeping the focus on yourself and removing your fears, allows you the opportunity to replace them with a peace you desperately desire. You can transform your past tragedies into present day and future seeds of triumph.

Twelve step programs will help you see things more objectively. Objective thinking can transform trash into treasure.

"Life is not a success-only journey." Dr. Phil

Not everyone is going to be on your cheer leading team. All the people you know will not always be encouraging you to change for the better, and succeed. This is a fact of life.

Does this fact force you to jump off the cliff right now? Is your life all about other people liking you? Someone created television remotes to change the channel. Get to a place in your life where you enjoy your own company enough to gently detach from people who do not have your best interest at heart. Change the channel and turn off your ears to their poisonous fears.

How can you begin to detach and let go?

Imagine a woman behind you yelling and cursing with displeasure in the grocery store. You could offer her the opportunity to go ahead of you in line. Transform her upside down frown into a right side up smile. The man who rudely pushes into you on the street corner? Pick up the things he dropped out of his bag, silently, speaking without words but actions. The family member that blames you for every problem in his/her life? Don't take it personally. What comes out of someone else's mouth is a reflection on them. What comes out of your mouth is a reflection of you.

"Preach always, and only when necessary, use words." St. Francis of Assisi

How do you know an apple tree is an apple tree? How do you know an oak tree is an oak tree? How do you know a banana tree is a banana tree?

The type of fruit it produces, of course! In the same way, a twelve step program will help teach you how to identify people and situations more honestly, so can you make better decisions and choices in all areas of your life.

In other words, when you learn how to identify the fruit (the behavior), you can clearly judge what kind of tree (the person) you are dealing with. This knowledge is a powerful tool; you can always use it to make better choices, choices that will help you to be happier.

The Bible contains some of the most modern day solutions to any of your everyday problems. Why?

Because it is filled with examples of human nature, more than two thousand years of good and bad behavior, decisions, outcomes, lessons, and a variety of wisdom.

This good book offers the simplest solutions to the most complex questions. It describes more helpful tools to maintain your happiness than any *New York Times* bestseller you could hope to find.

The "know a tree by its fruit,' is a direct formula taken right out of the Bible. It's simple, easy to understand, and highly accurate. This analogy is a great metaphor for many things in life.

You know a policeman is policeman by the uniform he wears. A fireman wears a fireman suit. A nun wears a habit. In the same way, dishonest people usually have a fruit of a lie, a person who loves you will deliver a fruit of respect, and people who genuinely care about you, usually express fruits of caring behavior. Want to know more about the truth of a person? Look at what he/she has done in their life.

Words are meaningless, all that matters is the action.

Anyone can say they love and care about you. If they beat you up, and steal your money, they are a liar. This is the truth.

You can only trust the truth of a statement by the action behind the words. If you want to enjoy the benefits of a twelve step program, I will only believe you when you show me you've gone to a meeting.

What twelve step meeting might you attend?

Pray about which one might be the best match for you. Remember, "Twelve step programs are not allied with any sect, denomination, political entity, organization, or institution: they do not engage in any controversy, neither endorse nor oppose any cause. There are no dues for membership. They are self supporting through voluntary contributions." *12 Step Program Guide*

AL-ANON and AL-ATEEN:

www.al-anon.alateen.org

As you may have noticed, this group is my personal favorite. It is also the one group I firmly believe could benefit anyone. Perhaps this fellowship could be named, "The twelve steps for everyone."

Most people who have a loved one, or anyone they care about, who is an alcoholic, has probably experienced other types of dysfunctional behavior as well. Is it just me, or does most of the world seem to fit this dysfunctional description?

Al-Anon is designed to help families of alcoholics. This means that if you know you have a family member, or a friend, who is an alcoholic, Al-Anon is available to support you. Available to help you deal with the effects the alcoholic is having on YOU.

Are you perhaps thinking, "How do I define an alcoholic, and how do I know if I've been affected by one?"

Most people believe they know someone who occasionally drinks. Often these people appear to be free of any overpowering compulsion to drink at inappropriate times, and probably seem to function well in every day life. Is this a problem drinker?

The second question may be, "I am not sure alcoholism is in my family history, but know I/they experienced dysfunction (i.e., sexual abuse, physical abuse, drug use, gambling, etc.)." "Can Al-Anon still help me?"

If you think either of these situations may apply to you, it probably does. If you think one of your parents drank too much some or all of the time, Al-Anon offers something that can help you. The person could be grandparent, brother, sister, close friend, boyfriend, girlfriend, husband, wife, cousin, or even your boss.

Anyone who was/is important and active in your world can have an effect on you.

It doesn't matter if you are aware that a different type of problem or dysfunction is/was more predominant in your life. The effects of alcohol were/are still some part of your life experience. Yes, Al-Anon can help you, too.

Obvious examples of stereotypical alcoholics are easy to find, but what about the other people you know who drink and seem to be normal? How do you distinguish between the normal drinker, and the problem drinker? After all, if you're not sure it's a problem for them, how do you know if it's been a problem for you?

Imagine you grew up in a family where mom and dad enjoyed their cocktails only at social gatherings. You can, however, remember more than a few times where they came home a bit drunk. Although infrequently, existence of the situation, probably still earns you a membership ticket into the Al-Anon program.

Perhaps your husband or wife indulges only a few times a month in alcohol. Although these times are infrequent, the level of indulgence is severe. He or she may not be able to drive home, forgets things they said, or conducts crazy behaviors they do not remember. You too, may be a card carrying member waiting to activate your Al-Anon membership.

If you're a friend or relative of someone who has admitted to having had a drinking problem in the past, does not regularly attend an

AA program, or proudly claims they are cured, you may get help out of the Al-Anon program. Even if the alcoholic is not actively drinking, left untreated, the effects of the alcoholic are still active and affecting you today.

This concept may be very difficult to understand and accept. "How can someone who has stopped drinking, continue to release alcoholic effects on me?"

There is no graduation from alcoholism or its effects. There is only progress, and transformation, in the process of recovery.

Imagine you are allergic to clams or scallops (like me). You know that within fifteen minutes of eating any one those mollusk family members, you will quickly be in excruciating pain, experiencing a most glamorous event of puking your guts out for hours. In just fifteen minutes, your body has gone from calm to chaotic.

What have you learned? You understand if you do not eat scallops or clams, you go on living a physically normal life. If you do not eat clams or scallops, then you will not experience unwanted pain and suffering.

Do you think this allergic reaction is time sensitive? No, you accept that this reaction is in your blood. Months, even years may go by, and you are perfectly safe from this allergic reaction, and sorrow. But as soon as you eat a clam or scallop, wham! The same huge chain reaction immediately occurs once again.

Why is it that all those years can go by without a single problem, and now you are still susceptible to the allergic reaction? Because it's in your blood, it's part of who you are, and will be until the day you die. The point is, you can be perfectly fine, living a perfectly normal life, if you do not eat clams or scallops. You feel no shame in accepting this fact. You simply understand that you can not eat clams and scallops in your diet without getting severely physically sick.

The same is true with alcoholism. If a person knows he or she is an alcoholic, and treats the disease with a good twelve step, AA program, their life can most likely go on without too many adverse effects.

A person, who knows he or she has a problem with alcoholism, and does not take the recovery medicine, is a bomb waiting to explode. Negative behaviors, despite the absence of alcohol, are still alive and well. Who will receive the effects of these negative behaviors? Who is receiving maximum exposure to them? The answer could be you.

Perhaps you feel it is unfair that if you know the other person has a problem with alcoholism, you need to go to a twelve step program yourself. The world is not fair, only God is fair.

The answer is simple: you have a problem too. You have been affected by their problem, which now makes it your problem.

They love the alcohol, and you love them.

It can be frightening to admit you could be subconsciously seeking the abuse that comes with an alcoholic relationship. That you spend time attracted to people you want to fix, or want to help.

Why do you want to spend so much time and effort fixing other people?

Could it be, perhaps, that this obsession keeps you so busy, you do not have time to look at all the things YOU need to fix inside yourself? Your self esteem has been shattered so badly in the past, being surrounded by insanity is familiar to you. The past conflicts and chaos has turned your mind upside down with confusion.

Confusion is not of God. Peace is the fruit of being with God. If you experience confusion and lack peace, the Al-Anon program can help you rewire your mind right side up.

AA:

www.aa.com

Webster's dictionary defines alcohol as, "Caused by, or containing alcohol. A person affected with alcoholism. Continued, excessive, and uncontrollable use of alcoholic drinks. A complex chronic psychological and nutritional disorder associated with such use."

Do you find yourself saying, "I need a drink" to deal with something? Do you say to yourself, "I won't have more than one or two drinks," and regret having gone through the whole six pack or bottle of wine, all by yourself? Have you been stopped for drunk driving? Do you plan events or your schedule around when you can kick back and have a few cocktails? Do you repeatedly say to yourself during your day, "I can't wait to get home and have a drink?" Do you find it impossible to imagine your life without alcohol, ever again?

The above website contains a list of questions you can ask yourself to determine if you have a problem with your drinking, and how a twelve step program can help you. It is reasonable to deduce, if you think you have a problem with your drinking, that you probably do.

Don't waste one more minute thinking, "Maybe I'll go to an AA meeting someday." Do not delay; just go.

Another hangover is not going to miraculously provide the happiness you so desperately seek. Do not avoid the truth. Only the truth can set you free.

Why do want to procrastinate on going to an AA meeting? Procrastination rhymes with assassination for a reason. The only person you're killing by delaying is you. Embrace the help offered, the same way you enjoy going on a plane for a happy vacation. Resistance is futile. There is no shame in accepting help for a problem you do not know how to fix.

Perhaps it is time to give up control. Take off your super character costume. The one you wear with the big "P" in the middle for pride. Swallow the medication that will make you well with a spoon full of sugar, if it helps it go down.

AL-ATEEN:

www.al-anon.alateen.org

I wish and pray every teenager who suffers the rampant disease of our dysfunctional upside down world, would attend Al-Ateen.

How great would it be to have known about all these tools at a younger age? How much pain and suffering could have been avoided? What healthier choices could you have made? What would your life look like with this earlier cure? How fabulous would it have been to get this preventative care? How much positive energy could have taken root in the garden of life? How much happier, and peaceful could you have been?

Yes, this is a group specifically devoted to the needs of our terrific teens. Young people who may be dealing with the effects of alcohol, drugs, or any type of human dysfunction.

Having worked with teenagers for years, I believe that these young people intuitively feel when something is upside down.

The problem remains in their not understanding how to fix what they know is wrong. They often feel there is no way to make the situation any better. The have not been taught how to turn the upside down into the right side up. They believe there is no choice for them to make. All they can envision is the shadow of a green sky lurking beside them every day.

The teenagers in this program encourage each other to change for the happier. They provide each other support to stop the landslide of destructive behavior. They share personal experience and success, and provide inspirational examples of how to avoid wasting time in other people's destructive lives.

Peers sharing similar challenges, listen to one another in a non-judgmental way. These teens want to stop their negative upside down world, and turn their lives right side up peaceful, purposeful, and happy. What a testimony!

Do you know someone who desires to be a terrific teen? Could you be a role model and catalyst for positive change? Can you be love in action and take them to a meeting in your town today?

Today's world is tough for anyone, at any age. Teens are now engaging in rampant self destructive behaviors such as cutting, damaging new strength drugs, and self destructive sex at younger ages.

The media outlets desensitize these young people towards self esteem destruction. The internet, porn, lack of good role models, reinforces green sky thinking as a masquerade for true blue.

Be a blessing to a terrific teen and tell them about this support group. Investigate the website yourself; encourage them to go, drop them off at a meeting. Intervene and help them use time wisely. Inspire and motivate them. Nurture their desire through your love and active support. Help give them a chance to learn how to transform that bad hand of cards into a winning hand.

Perhaps it is upside down for you to believe our teenagers don't matter as much as adults do. They have no power or significance? They are our future leaders, CEO's, law makers, teachers, and presidents of tomorrow! They will someday be the majority of our society. Investing in their sanity and good self esteem, is an investment in everyone. The success or failure of our spiritual economy depends on these teens.

Many of us have done much damage to our youth through divorce, alcoholism, drugs, pornography, and the overall lack of genuine sacrificial love they deserve. We have contributed to their problems, and often lacked the self discipline or care, to contribute to being part of their solution. This is wrong.

Fortunately, like any disease, if diagnosed and treated early enough, a complete cure is often possible. The probability for successful treatment increases with early treatment.

Can you bring the gift of early treatment to a teen? Take them to an Al-Ateen meeting and make a positive difference.

SLAA:

www.slaafws.org

This group is filled with tough soldiers, fighting heavy combat.

You have seen some real tough times to be in this program. SLAA is the one twelve step program most people have never heard about, and ironically, the fellowship most people need. This disease is deeply misunderstood.

Bill O'Reilly talks about his own experience of falling into this upside down type of crazy mismatch with a woman who was very beautiful on the outside. She was also equally manipulative, and mean spirited on the inside.

"I actually thought I could change this woman," O'Reilly states. "That was insane." As a result of this personal experience, he concludes, "What society needs is a twelve step program for infatuated Americans. This organization would supply wise counselors when we are tempted to associate with those who would do us harm but look so good doing it. I'm not kidding."

Well, SLAA does exactly that.

Do you find yourself addicted to a person instead of a drug? Is this person like a drug for you? Do you know you need to leave a man or woman who treats you miserably, but continue to stay in this relationship? Are you on a constant merry-go-round of breaking up and getting back together, only to break up and get back together once again? Do you continue to maintain a destructive relationship that you know must absolutely go?

Are you cemented in a chair for hours in secret so you can experience a high from the porn you view? Do you plan your whole day around it? Do you want to stop but every time you promise yourself you will, you just stay for more?

Does the thought of ending relationships with these people, places, or things fill you with anxiety like withdrawal?

If any of the above sounds remotely familiar to you, you are not alone. SLAA – Sex and Love Addictions Anonymous - helps people like you. Similar to any other addiction, this disease turns the upside down of lust, into a counterfeit right side up of love.

Perhaps because this type of content is easy to access through media channels, sexy glamour on TV, and the internet, this disease has recently exponentially exploded.

I first heard about this disease when I had already been in the Al-Anon program for nearly two years. I was trying desperately to break off an engagement with a man who I knew was poison for me. It was impossible for me to separate, and I had many justifications for why I should give the relationship, "one more good try."

Eventually, when my life became bluntly unmanageable, I accepted that I needed help. Help for what, from where?

Al-Anon helped me get the strength and confidence to know I deserved better than this abusive relationship, but the backlash from that decision was more than I could have imagined, or prepared to bear.

My therapist directed me to read a book called, *Facing Love Addiction,* by Pia Melody (www.piamelody.com).

I devoured the words in days. The pages were alive! I never imagined this could be me. I found solace knowing I was not alone.

Hitting rock bottom, I was now more open to finding a meeting for this unique twelve step program. Here I found hope for my broken body, mind, and spirit. I learned how to set healthier boundaries, and learned this person had become my God. Why did I not want to let God be my God?

SLAA is very specifically targeted toward people who are feeling addicted to a person. This person could be you, through porn or masturbation. Typically, those with the disease are addicted to a person with whom they are having sex. Hence, the sex, and love addiction combination.

The upside down confusion, that sex equals love in our society, is overwhelming. Somewhere along the way, people like us never got the proper opportunity to connect love as an action word of sacrifice and concern. We got the message it as an action, just between the sheets.

The feeling of being abandoned from the person we have misunderstood as loving, is overpowering. No matter how much we want to let go, the task becomes physically, and emotionally impossible.

If you have been sexually abused in your past, you may be more vulnerable to this disease. In my case, I had been sexually abused by a high school teacher. Held hostage to this perversion throughout my high school years, this predator never went away until I went away to college.

A shameful secret, I carried it with me for many years. I was fourteen at the time, and I certainly had no idea what was truly happening. I only knew someone older, someone in authority, was paying attention to me, attention that made me feel special, important, loved. Or so I thought. Perhaps I longed for what I thought I was missing in my family at home. We all want to be loved.

A great place for teens to help them avoid the misconception that sex equals love is www.chastity.com. Created by Jason and Crystalina Evert, these people also offer their experience, strength, and hope to those young adults who want authentic love without lust. They have talked the walk, and walked the talk.

Jason travels the country speaking to young people. I have had the privilege to attend one of these events with a large group of teens.

Some of the teens I spoke with after the event shared their reactions, "Deb, hearing this has changed my life for the better. I will never be the same again."

Whole heartily dedicated to helping teens attain good self esteem, live with dignity, and make a positive difference with their peers, the Everts can turn any green sky to blue.

Do you have similar pain to share? Don't beat yourself up. You couldn't possibly have understood what was going on at that young age. You did the best you could at the time with the knowledge you had at the time. Forgive yourself. Forgive the predator. Sexual abuse is much more the responsibility of the adult.

You are only as sick as your secrets. SLAA can help set you free from this sick secret, starting today.

Left untreated, those old secrets effect your life today. The unhealed past only grows distorted thinking and feeling, today.

Use the tools in a twelve step program to transplant upside down lies into right side up truths. You will be much happier if you do.

You may want to investigate other twelve step programs such as: Codependents Anonymous, Adult Children of Alcoholics, Narcotics Anonymous, Emotions Anonymous, or anger management groups, to name a few. Try one or all of them.

Which one is right for you? Say a prayer, asking God to lead you to the right group for you, the program that brings you the most healing and happiness.

All of these twelve step programs work because they shift your focus from your pain, your addiction, that person or drug, towards a God, a Higher Power. This Higher Power is bigger, and more powerful, than your problem. You have to stop making any person, any drug, any displaced attachment, your God. You have to let go of the counterfeit God, to make room for the real God to guide you to genuine happiness.

As long as you care more about what people think, than what you and your God think, you will always be hostage to unhappiness.

I once upon a time, believed only a selfish, and arrogant God, would require me to place Him first. What kind of love is this? Does God not want me to have fun or enjoy pleasure? I thought only saints did that. "I don't want to be a saint!"

Now I know this demand from God, to put Him first in all matters, is unselfish and most loving.

When I put God first, and care more about what He thinks, including myself, I am accepting the peaceful truth I do not have complete control of my life. How does that help you?

When you are no longer under the control, power, or influence of another person, you are truly free. Why? Because whether other people like you or dislike you, agree with you or disagree, whatever other people think, has no effect on what you think, feel, say, or do.

You are no longer vulnerable, attached, or influenced in any decision by another person. Your inner value as a person does not depend on another person's outward opinion.

Awareness + Acceptance + Action = A happier you!

You + God = a winning majority combination!

Your happiness does not come from other peoples' minds. When this happens, you will no longer feel compelled to justify the actions of your life. You will no longer waste energy trying to bring another person over to your point of view. The ego of arrogance and insecurity no longer needs to be fed. You can feel good about yourself, and your decisions, with the help of God. Your need for other people's approval suddenly disappears.

How can you respect a different point of view, if you are tenaciously gripping your own? How can you be open to happier possibilities if you spend all your time, and energy defending the existence of a green sky?

Placing God first does not rob you of happiness. Placing God first is the very source of your happiness. Avalanche style!

Don't be afraid to try something new. Don't be afraid to go to a twelve step meeting. Believe anything is possible for you to accomplish, no matter any amount of good or bad in your past. You don't have to be an expert to get started.

Remember, "Amateurs built Noah's Ark and the professionals built the Titanic." Anonymous

This chapters Exercise:

Get yourself to a twelve step meeting as soon as possible.

CHAPTER V

PROFESSIONAL GUIDANCE –
THERAPISTS AND COACHES

Doesn't it seem to be the "in" thing today to talk about your therapist or coach?

Everyone seems to have one, from movie stars, to your next door neighbor. What was once a negative social taboo has suddenly become the pervasive norm, or even an exploding trend.

- Why would you want to go to a therapist or coach in the first place?
- How could a therapist or coach help you find your happiness faster and more effectively?
- How do you distinguish the difference between a good therapist or coach, and a bad one?

You must take the time to ask yourself these questions, before you know what's best for you. Your hope to find the correct answer with so many therapists and coaches available to you, how do you know who to select and trust? How do you discern who is most competent to provide the happiness you seek? Which therapist, or which coach, wastes your time, with no good results for you, but big successful results for their bank account?

Perhaps if we were all well adjusted, confident in ourselves, trusted our discernment, truly believed we were being guided by a divine loving God, had some trustworthy family, genuine selfless friends willing to share their personal wisdom, I'm not sure there would be such a thing known as professional therapy or coaching.

Unfortunately, an enormous amount of people living in our modern day times, have had to deal with very severe emotional dysfunctions. There have been too many lies and not enough truth.

People who do not know that they don't know everything, fight against keeping the focus on themselves, and do not believe in a loving God who unconditionally cares for them. They never stay silent long enough to pray, and are unaware free twelve step programs exist to heal their broken heart.

Everyone appears to be caught up in a solitary rat race. This circular activity of going no where of value fast, eliminates people's ability to actively listen, share, or advise with prudence.

Sad but true, most people are desperate to find someone who magically has all the correct answers to all their upside down problems in life. Who has the secret?

What do people do when they feel abandoned by friends, family, and God, to get the answers they want? They pay people money to buy the illusion of answers to relieve their internal pain. "Tell me what I think, please." Have you gone to a therapist, or coach, for such a reason as any of these?

Therapy is defined by Webster's as, "Treatment of bodily, mental, or behavioral disorders." Psychotherapy then, deals with the, "Treatment of mental or emotional disorder or of related bodily ills by psychological means."

The above definition clearly indicates the connection between the mind, body, and soul. Treat the mind, and it affects the body, which affects your entire soul.

Perhaps you were, or are, motivated to change because you are feeling enormous pain. Upside down thinking creates bad thoughts. Bad seeds only produce bad fruits. When you have a tree of rotting fruit that smells unbearable, you may be compelled to achieve relief.

You feel sick, tired, confused, anxious, out of energy, disinterested, and unable to find enthusiasm and purpose for living. You are surrounded by green clouds when you think a therapist or coach will fix all your problems.

"If I go to therapy, then I will get well." A therapist is not a quick fix store. You can't put a solution in a basket, buy it, and bring it home like your groceries.

A therapist or coach can only be a guide to help you find the travel plan you seek. He/she can only give you a map according to the destination you tell him/her you want to find. They can only give you what you want, depending if he/she has it to give you. A therapist or coach can not carry you to where you want to go. Your walking into the life you want will never come upon a therapist or coaches set of legs.

All a good therapist or coach can do is to help you define more clearly what you want, and offer objective new insight as to why you perhaps have not already gotten to where you want to be. They may know about, and share, fresh new tools that can help you build your new home on Happiness Island, but they are definitely not going to build it for you.

"You can lead a horse to water, but you can't make him drink." Unknown

A good therapist can lead you to the water, but only you can decide to take the action of wisdom drinking the healthy knowledge into your soul.

There are good and bad in every profession of life. Therapists and coaches are not exempt from this rule.

If a good tree produces good fruit, and a bad tree produces bad fruit, believe this fact: a bad therapist will produce bad results and only a good therapist can provide good results.

Do not go to the hardware store for bread!

I have personally experienced both a good therapist, and a bad therapist. The differences between them, the results they can offer, are unquestionably shocking.

What do you need to know?

- A good therapist will encourage you to engage in finding sources of growth for you outside the therapy session. An example of this might be the therapist that suggests you attend a good twelve step program between therapy sessions, recommend a book, or listen to a specific CD. A bad therapist will encourage you to limit your source of help to him/her in the therapy sessions solely.
- A good therapist will have a Higher Power or God they rely on for their own direction and discernment. A bad therapist will not talk about a higher power, attempting to convince you *they* are your higher power.
- A good therapist will not talk about his/her own problems during the therapy session. A bad therapist will tell you all about their personal life situation, and freely incorporate their own problems into a significant portion of your therapy session.

- A good therapist will be free of any lawsuit. This could be boundary infringements or other client/therapist privacy privilege. A bad therapist will have engaged in one or more legal accusations or law suits.
- A good therapist will suggest some type of homework assignment for you between sessions. A good therapist will measure progress, and maintain forward momentum towards recovery. A bad therapist will not suggest doing or reflection on specific growth issues between sessions.
- A good therapist will have detailed notes on you, your issues, your progress, and the good work you've done. A bad therapist will not have client notes beyond those required for legal or insurance purposes.
- A good therapist will fill you with a deep feeling of peace, comfort, and hope upon departure of the session. A bad therapist will leave you feeling confused, agitated, and weak.
- A good therapist reinforces that therapy is, "a process." There is no magic pill, no quick fix, and no graduation to learning in the experience of life.

"All of life is an experiment." Ralph Waldo Emerson

You are only given this present moment. That is why it is known as a present. A gift that you have with the breath you now take. You are not finished yet. Happiness is around the corner for you!

"The road to happiness is the journey itself." Anonymous

You can make progress without having to do it perfectly. Could one of your imperfections be that you have to do something perfectly, or it is not worth doing at all? "Perfect," is a green sky illusion, which no longer serves a good purpose for you.

A therapist or coach can guide you towards right side up changes in yourself. Good changes in you automatically changes the world around you. Don't give up five minutes before the miracle!

Eliminate any false expectation that going to therapy will relieve all painful feelings from sorrowful events in your life. False expectations are premeditated disappointments. What you will be able to change is how well, how fruitful, and how enjoyable the process of changing will be, from this moment forward.

You are going somewhere in your life. You are going one of two places; towards what you want, or away from what you don't want. The key that unlocks your door to happiness is accepting that you are definitely going somewhere, with every thought, action, and decision you make. No decision is a decision itself.

Do you want to be involved in the direction of your life? Do you want to go towards the passions and desires you have dreamed to achieve? Do you want to enjoy the process of getting there?

"I find the great thing in this world is not so much where we should stand, as in what direction we are moving." Oliver Wendell Holmes

You have already changed the direction of your course by your initial desire to change it. You want to dig your feet deep into the sand of peace beach. Feel the healing rays of the sunshine that soak your soul on Happiness Island. You have decided you are worth the effort.

"It is good to have an end to journey towards, but it is the journey itself that matters in the end." Ursula LeGuin

"Seed – Time – Harvest," are natural laws that contain living truth for everything under the sun. All of nature works on the basis of this simple, three step principal. This truth also applies to you.

Can you put an oak tree seed in the ground, walk in your house, and expect to go back outside one hour later and find a full grown twenty foot oak tree? Why do expect this type of quick result from yourself? Why do beat yourself up because you think you don't get it yet? Why do you put that type of pressure on yourself? This incorrect equation of seed and harvest without the necessary component of time, is an equation for unhappiness. Get rid of it!

Plant a seed, give it time, and a harvest will result.

The key here is: give it time. It takes time for things to happen, both good and bad. Every action has a result, and every choice has a consequence.

It is imperative that you contemplate with active awareness the type of seeds you are planting in your life. Why? Because those seeds are predetermined to give you back a predetermined result. Good seeds produce good results, which can lead you to happiness. Bad seeds produce bad results, leading you to despair.

Does an apple tree grow potatoes? Do dogs give birth to people? Do fish eggs produce birds? Pine trees do not grow into palm trees. Roses don't bloom tulips, and sheep don't bark.

Good seeds of happiness planted in the garden of your life produce peace and joy.

Your good thoughts, beliefs, and actions, produce good results in you. Negative actions produce negative results. You may not see these results today, this year, or even the year after that. But eventually, I promise you, all the good and bad you do in this life comes back to you, returning like a powerful boomerang, in the same measure you give, you receive.

Have you ever done something nice for someone, and at the time you didn't think much about it? Days, months or even years later, somehow that person or a friend of that person unexpectedly comes back into your life. They surprise you by sharing that you made a positive difference in their life. Your actions from so long ago grew positive results in their life today. You may barely remember what it was you did for them, but they have not forgotten the good lasting fruit you helped produce for them to enjoy.

Have you ever done something to someone that you regret? Did you think no one would ever find out about your terrible deed? Did you feel you made a safe escape from experiencing the consequences? Were you convinced you got away with it? Did you feel the bad action did not truly matter, justified by the fact you would never see them again?

Wham! By some bizarre sequence of events beyond your control, you find yourself working for that person. Or you discover that this person is now dating your best friend. Perhaps they've become your new next door neighbor. Just when you thought you were safe, the past is back.

Whatever you do, given time, will produce a result. It's unavoidable, like your very own shadow. Once you can accept this truth, you will effortlessly be open to change for the happier.

A good therapist or coach should help you pause to make better choices in your life.

Fixing the immediate problem you want solved, is not going to fix the problem that brought you to the problem in the first place. Changing the thought pattern at the root of the problem will allow you to identify potential seeds for this problem you don't want to grow again.

"Catch a man a fish, he eats for a day, teach a man to fish, he eats for a lifetime." Anonymous

You don't want a therapist that catches fish for you; you want a therapist who teaches you how to fish.

A good therapist will help you stop wanting to go to the hardware shop for a loaf of bread.

Is it upside down thinking for you to believe, after one hundred trips to the hardware store looking for a loaf of bread, that you will eventually find the loaf of bread there? Do you believe on your one hundred and first trip to the hardware store, the miracle of the loaves will appear to feed the five thousand?

What do you do?

You stop for a moment, think about what you need, and then make a choice as to where you can best find it.

The problem is not the hardware store; it's you for going to the hardware store looking for a loaf of bread. What part of you stubbornly insists the hardware store sell you a loaf of bread? Why do you not want to go to the grocery store, where you know there are hundreds of loaves of bread to buy? Is it the hardware store's fault you should have been smart enough to go the grocery store to find that loaf of bread?

A good therapist will help teach you how to think through the consequences of your choices, all your decisions. A good therapist will help you go to the hardware store for hardware, and the grocery store for the loaf of bread. A good therapist will help you understand that upside down thinking will only produce a frustrating, upside down result. Acceptance and surrender will no longer feel like failure, but freedom.

A good therapist or coach can be a positive punctuation mark in your life. A positive mentor to help you pause a moment, consider all your options, all the many possibilities available to you.

"How might I feel about this result, of this choice, five years from now? What other results might occur from this choice ten or fifteen years from now? What about if I died tomorrow? Will I regret doing this, or might I regret not doing it?"

Think it through, spiral it down to the best possible result, or the worst case scenario. After this reflection, make a choice, and let go of the result. Know you did the best you could to make a good decision, at that time, with the information you had to investigate. You're sky is getting more blue today!

"Wise people increase their opportunity for success by taking the time to objectively review all the potential positives and negatives, and then take deliberate action forward." Ben Franklin

Make your own two-columned, Ben Franklin list.

Write down both the good and the bad. Everything has a good and bad attached. Make a list for yourself, and imagine how you will feel if everything on the list, good or bad, should actually happen. Then you will know what to do.

We often create our own problems in our lives when we expect a different result from the same failed behavior. You have to do something different to get a different result.

Your best thinking got you here; your best thinking is not going to get you out of here, so you must try something new.

Place yourself around people, and in situations, that are already achieving your dream of happiness. People who know where to buy seeds of happiness, plant seeds of happiness, grow a fragrant field of happiness.

No one can give what they don't already have themselves, including a therapist or coach.

Have you ever gone boating or sailing?

If you have, you know you have to plot a course to get where you want to go. You also know being off course by a small amount of five degrees in the beginning, if left unchanged, you will inevitably have catastrophic results. The longer you remain off course, the larger the degree off course you will be, given more time, and distance you travel.

In the beginning, five degrees off course does not appear to be a big deal. It truly does not have to be. What do you have to do to avoid the potential bad result? You must be aware, quickly notice you are off track, and promptly readjust your course.

What motivates you to readjust your course right away? Experience proves five degrees off course now, can be fifty degrees off later. Who suffers the consequence of letting the boat continue of course? You.

This knowledge allows you to make a choice.

Do you readjust course now, where you lose only a small amount of time to find your destination? Or do you let the boat continue off course and passively accept the destination you find, like it or not? Do you want to take the risk?

Imagine that boat trip is your whole life.

You may have gotten off course to Happiness Island because you didn't know what you now know. You innocently kept on going in the same bad direction, increasing the mathematical distance between where you are, and where you want to be.

At some point in your life, you noticed you were off course. You wanted to walk under the blue sky on peace beach, and instead found yourself under the green sky of confusion city.

Catch being off course early on and you will not have to suffer greater bad consequences of being off course later on. An error in the beginning is an error indeed. Examine where you are in your course towards happiness.

"The unexamined life is not worth living." Aristotle

Thinking about what you are thinking about, could be the modern day version of Aristotle's famous phrase. A good therapist or coach can help you add tools in your tool box to build this examined happy life.

Years ago, Bishop Fulton Sheen, had a hit TV show, *Life Is Worth Living!* That includes YOU, and your life, too.

A good therapist, or coach, will help you become the best person God created you to be.

Your good therapist or coach, knows it is not in your best interest, or for the people around you, to try to make you into something else other than what you were gifted to be. Changing you to be like someone else is another trip to the hardware store for bread.

You must be uniquely yourself to be truly happy. No one has ever been, or ever will be, uniquely you. There is no right or wrong to being you. What is right or wrong for you is indicated by the amount of peace, or confusion, you produce.

Does a daffodil complain it wants to be a rose?

A daffodil is a daffodil for a reason, and a rose is a rose for a reason. Just because they are different, does not mean one type of flower is better than the other.

Many people may love roses, and feel daffodils are ugly. Many other people absolutely adore daffodils, and think roses are totally unattractive. This is just an opinion, not a truth.

If you're a daffodil, don't try to be a rose. Roses, don't try to be a daffodil. Focus on the fact, and be happy to know you are a beautiful flower. If you need some positive reinforcement about the truth of your beauty as a daffodil, don't try to find solace from all the people you know adore roses. Find the daffodil fans for support. What if you do come across a rose lover, who tells you he/she thinks you are the ugliest flower on earth? Believe in your heart that one opinion does not effect, or change, the opinion of all the many daffodil fans. Authentic fans will treasure you just the way you are.

"Think for yourself, and let others enjoy the privilege of doing so too." Voltaire

Imagine we are all a piece in the puzzle called life.

Each person can contribute a small piece to this puzzle, but a critical piece to creating the entire picture. Without your special piece of the puzzle in the picture, the picture can never be complete.

A good therapist or coach can help you determine the shape of your puzzle piece. Can work with you in the search to find where you fit in the bigger picture called life. The picture is endless. Everything that ever was, and ever is, has been meticulously planned on this magnificent mural. Without every brush stroke, without every piece of puzzle placed where intended, gaps of empty space would abound. Who will fill those one of a kind shaped spaces now?

You are a very special piece of the picture, intentionally and carefully designed, to be of a specific purpose to the big picture of all time. Do not waste precious time trying to fit yourself in a place where you were never designed to go! Spend your time, and energy, enjoying the search of discovering where you were designed to fit.

Focus on an attitude of gratitude that you have been entrusted with a specific piece of a masterpiece. Now you're starting to look for bread in the grocery store!

A good therapist will help you look at the upside down things in your life with a spirit of hope. He/she will help you find places where you can turn your pile of manure into rich, useful fertilizer. A good therapist can help you transform the most poisonous curses in your life into the most powerful healing cures in your life.

Winter arrives in New England, and all the trees are bare. If you had not grown up here to witness the transformation, you might assume all the trees were forever dead. Is there any evidence in the present moment to prove otherwise? Surely, these trees are hopelessly dead.

Then, as time goes on, spring arrives. Without any help from you, all the trees that appeared once dead are now transformed into life again! Suddenly, without notice, hundreds of small green buds have opened to become lush green leaves. What could be more alive than these?

You have a tree of life too, sparking special shine known as – you!

What looks upside down and dead, is in fact, right side up, and alive. The environment, the weather conditions, the temperature just needed to change, to bring the reality into tangible view. There never was anything wrong with the tree when it had leaves, or was looking dead bare. It was still the same tree inside, no matter how it appeared in winter or spring. Your own tree of life is no different.

Life contains some spicy seasonings, better known as mistakes or at least what appear to be mistakes at the time. Life also contains many delicious deserts, better known as good decisions, or at least what appear to be at the time. The critical element that determines the end of the story is, given time.

Pencils have erasers attached to them for a reason.

You have an eraser attached to you, too. That eraser is called forgiveness. How do you know if you are forgiving? Take the thermometer test. The more you are able to forgive the faults of others is a direct reflection of how much you forgive yourself. If you are stubborn to forgive others, you are stubborn to forgive yourself. Forgiving other people is not about them, it's about you. How much do you, or how much don't you, love, and forgive yourself? The more you forgive yourself, the more you genuinely forgive those around you.

Upside down thinking believes forgiveness is about them, the other people. Right side up vision, clearly see's it is truly about me.

"He who does not forgive, digs two graves." Chinese Proverb

When you stop taking arsenic, and expect the other person to die, you are beginning to forgive. You are beginning to let go of the resentment weeds, making space for flowers of forgiveness to grow.

A good therapist or coach should help you prune yourself. What does this mean? You need to prune away dead areas of your life, the same way a rose bush needs to be pruned in the fall season to reach full bloom in the season of spring. Prune away branches of self hatred and resentments towards others. New growth can be strong branches of good virtues, love, and healthy self-esteem.

I will be the first to admit pruning hurts, but it works.

You can not allow unhealthy growth to run rampant, without simultaneously sucking the life away from the healthy growth. If you do not prune the unhealthy growth off some of the plant, you will encourage greater deformity in the entire plant. This results in severe ugliness the following season. Keeping the longer protruding branches is upside down, cutting back all the branches to a shorter, stronger, compact size, is right side up.

Pruning yourself hurts now, but later on promises happier results of beauty, and joy. A good therapist and coach can help show you what, and where, you need to prune. The upside down thought that you have been holding on to some apparently good parts of yourself, may be keeping you deformed. You're going to have to let some of those branches you think you like go, in order to get the full experience of the happiness you seek. You are worth the effort!

A good therapist can help you fine tune, and mature your God given intuition. Increasing your ability to discern good from bad allows you to make better choices. All of us have what is commonly known as a gut instinct. "Something told me not to trust that person." "I don't know why I like that person, I just know I do." "I have a bad feeling about that situation, I don't know why."

If you grew up in a dysfunctional home, especially around alcoholism, drugs or verbal abuse, you were taught to turn off that intuitive ability system.

Perhaps you came home from being out with you friends one night, and you found your mother dragging your father upstairs to bed. Dad passed out on the couch from drinking too much earlier in the evening.

"Mom, what's wrong with dad, what happened?"

Your mother comments, "Oh nothing dear, everything is just fine. Go up to bed. I'll see you in the morning."

Well, of course something is wrong! Your father was dead drunk, and now your mother is struggling to get him upstairs to bed. Your eyes, mind, and common sense tell you, by virtue of the very scene you're witnessing, that something is definitely wrong. But, the message you hear from your loving and trusting mother, is "everything is fine." You hear these conflicting words as you simultaneously view this dysfunctional scene, which is clearly not fine. Everything looks wrong, but you're hearing everything is right.

What do you think this does to your mind? Boot camp training for upside down insanity, stinking thinking!

You see something you know in your heart to be true, but you are told something completely different. Given enough repetition over time, you'll start changing your thinking to accommodate what the authority figure is telling you to be true, instead of believing the truth you feel deep inside, which you know to be true.

"Well, there must be something wrong with me then," is the only possible answer that can balance out this broken equation. Hence, the destructive quest to prove to yourself there is indeed something wrong with YOU has begun. From here on in, you never completely trust your gut instinct to be entirely accurate ever again.

What does this grow?

You mislabel bad things as good, and good things as bad. Your upside down is right side up. Your sky is green, and your grass is blue. You're personal radar system, intuition, divine discernment, is stunted from growing right side up, and turned off. Without this healthy intuition to guide you through your precious, tender childhood and teenage years, you get lost in confusion city. You bring this distorted vision system into your adulthood, and wonder, "Why do I always attract these crazy, drama king/queen people, into my life?"

A good therapist or coach, twelve step program participation, praying, and keeping the focus on yourself with an open mind that you don't know everything, is going to turn that God given skill set back on!

What happens when something isn't used for awhile?

It becomes a bit squeaky, a tad rusty, works well inconsistently?

What do you now do?

You take the item to someone you know can fix it. Depending upon how long it wasn't used, or how many parts can be salvaged, will determine how long it will take to get the item fixed. A good mechanic or carpenter will most likely be able to fix whatever the problem. Given patience and time, a skilled technician can get almost anything working as good as new.

Your divine discernment and intuition are a bit rusty, too.

Oil and lubrication are necessary to get them working again. You might even need a few new parts. Fixing your divine discernment, will allow you to navigate towards happiness, and break through the black junk around the diamond of you. Never give up!

Exercise:

When you are in the presence of a person you have just met, take a moment to do your own personal body scan.

- How are you feeling as you stand next to this person?
- Do you feel something heavy in your gut?
- Do you feel something agitating you as you are talking with this person?
- Do you feel calm and peaceful when you hear this person's voice?
- Does confusion fill you head?

These feelings are numbers on your personal internal thermometer telling you how you truly feel, and are giving you a stop sign to assess the situation before you take further action.

If a person brings up confusion, and anxiety, run as fast as you can away from them. If you're feeling peace and serenity, stay and wait a little while, there may be something good this person can bring to you.

A good therapist or coach will always help you find something good in anything that appears to be bad. Something positive, something you can learn, and take away from any given situation.

However things seem to be going, always ask your higher power, "God, what can I learn from this?"

This is school, earth school, and no one here is staying forever. If you want to be happy, to be at peace, to feel deep joy, you must be willing to learn, to change, and grow for the better.

Green skies and blue grass do not have to be upside down facts in your life anymore.

Take your problems to God, but leave the solutions and timetable up to Him.

Are you excited to find a good therapist or coach, a mentor to help you unleash your personal best?

Interview your potential therapist or coach before you entrust this person with the source of life in your heart.

Consider asking him/her the following questions:

1. Do you believe in a higher power or God?
2. Do you recommend any type of twelve step program to your clients?
3. Do you offer reading or homework assignments to your clients between sessions?
4. Do you or have you had any legal claims filed against you?
5. How do you define "successful" therapy/coaching?
6. What is the result you would want me to expect from having come to see you?

The last one – is something you have to ask yourself.

7. "How do I feel in presence of this therapist and/or coach? Deep inside, do I feel agitated and more confused, or do I feel peaceful and hopeful?"

Did your employer hire you without a thorough interview? Did you get a paycheck for not working? Why then, should you pay a therapist or coach to do a job without interviewing them? You are more precious than the work you do.

When you look in the mirror, who do you see?

You see yourself, BUT you see yourself in reverse. We see a reflection of ourselves that is somewhat different from how we truly look to the world. Ambulance is written upside down backwards, to look right side up clear, in your rear view mirror.

Other people, like a good therapist or coach, can be a tool to eliminate the mirror. To see the truth of whom you really are.

Consider **The Gorilla Story**. Dan Simmons did this research study on perception at the University of Illinois.

He tells the audience he is going to show them a video clip of children passing balls. He explains that one group of kids will be wearing red shirts, the other white. He asks one half of the audience to focus on how many times the children wearing the red shirts pass the ball to one another, and asks the other half of the audience to do the same with the kids in the white shirts. He shows the video.

At the end of the video he asks each group how many times the children passed the ball to each other. Ten, fifteen, some said even eighteen times. He asked them if they noticed anything else unusual. Very few responded.

Then, he tells the entire group to watch the same video with no expectation. He tells them not to focus on counting the number of times the children pass the ball. Just watch the video without expectation.

At first, nothing appears to be different. The kids are passing the balls to each other, exactly as before. Suddenly, without warning, this huge man in a gorilla suit jumps into the middle of the children's circle and starts dancing around like a crazy gorilla!

The audience is roaring with laughter! You know why, don't you? Because, as the instructor demonstrated, we all have eyes that do not see, and minds that do not move. The audience was so influenced by the directive of the authority figure, the instructor, to follow directions to count the number of passes the children were making with the ball, they did not even notice that a huge man in a gorilla suit jumped into the middle of the picture!

Don't miss the obvious. Don't let someone else who may know far less than you, tell you who you are.

Don't let your happiness come from other people's minds.

No one in this world (except God of course), knows you better than you. Trust yourself with the help of your Higher Power to guide you in finding a good therapist or coach, a person who will help you become the best person you can be.

"We do not retreat from reality, we rediscover it." C.S. Lewis

CHAPTER VI

SURROUND YOURSELF IN TRANSFORMATION – MEDIA TOOLS

You have to think about, what you're thinking about.

- How can you cement this pathway to your peace and happiness?
- What will make reading this book a permanent event for genuine transformation?
- Where can you find daily vitamins to maintain a healthy, happy mind?

Surrounding yourself in transformation tools is easy, fun, and accessible for everyone. Good vitamins can be found on TV, the radio, internet, radio, or CD's. Imagine each media tool is a different type of vitamin, offering you focused strength that will enhance and maintain your overall well being, and happiness.

"How can what I see or hear, transform me into a happier person?"

Have you ever gone to scary movies? You sit through two hours of the horror show like *The Exorcist*, and how do you feel? How do you feel when you return home to your dark house and fumble to find the light switch? A little afraid? Do you keep one eye over your shoulder, waiting for the goolies to jump out and get you?

What caused you to feel so afraid?

The environment created in your mind during the events of the two hour horror show. The intake of what you saw and what you heard, created how you felt in the space of that two hour time period. Wherever you go, there you are, and you brought your frightening feelings home with you.

If watching a movie for only two hours, can affect you in such a tangible way, how much more are you affected by the repetitive things you see, hear, think, or say, constantly, everyday?

What you see and hear has a direct effect on how you feel, think, and act.

Make your life a fun, happy movie, and throw out that old horror show.

Achieving the happiness you seek, depends then, on exposing yourself to positive people, places, and things that create happiness. If you surround yourself in places of peace, gratitude, and hope, you will automatically grow happiness. Making a deliberate choice to seek out those happy producing environments, will inevitably grow a positive, happy result.

If you stand next to a pile of manure all day long, but you don't touch it, do you smell like manure at the end of the day? If you stand next to someone who is spraying beautiful fragrant perfume all over herself, and you are standing next to her, do you walk away smelling like perfume too? In either case, did you actually place manure or perfume directly on you? No. Then why do you pick up the fragrance of both simply by standing next to them?

You are whom you associate with. You attract what you are. Like associates with like. Sheep don't hang out with wolves, snakes don't sleep with rabbits, and the devil does not spend free time socializing with God.

How do you get the good information you want to know into your head? How do you surround yourself in the fragrant perfume of happiness? How do you walk on green grass, and not blue?

Did you ever watch the movie, *The Matrix*? Do you remember the scene where Trinity sat back in her chair, and information was downloaded into her brain, teaching her how to fly a helicopter? Do you remember how long that download took? Perhaps one full minute, to learn years of expert helicopter flying skills. That type of learning only happens in a movie, a science fiction movie at that.

What is the truth about how to learn something new, for you?

You must get the information into your head, but not through the input of a cd into your brain. You must read the information, listen to the information, watch the information, or experience the information that you want to learn. Somehow, the targeted information has to get into your mind to create the desired new action. This leaves you with two eyes, one mouth, and two ears to get the job successfully accomplished.

What do you think happens to your mind, body, and spirit if you constantly watch, read, and listen to negative news, violent television programming, or angry negative people. What do you think you are having to process? What result do you believe these negative seeds will grow in the fabric of your soul? How can bad seeds produce good results?

"Well, just a bit of that in my life doesn't do me any harm." Wrong! I don't think so!

I heard this story on a talk show one morning on, *Joni* (www. daystar.com). I call it **The Brownie Story**.

"One day, a mom and her children were discussing why it was important to be careful about what they watched on television, looked up on the Internet, and listened to on the radio. The kids, of course, complained, "everyone else does it." For some reason, the old cliché' about "if everyone jumped off the bridge, does that mean you have to do it, too," just didn't seem to be making an impact. So Mom, in her frustration, decided to take a break from the topic and change the focus to something less confrontational.

"Why don't we make some brownies together?" she shared with enthusiasm.

Of course, her children loved the idea, and began to run to find all the ingredients needed for the project. Eggs, sugar, a lot of chocolate, all those delicious things needed to create the best yummy brownies in the neighborhood.

After pouring the batter into the baking pan, the children left, and went outside to play. Looking forward to returning inside when the brownies were finally cooked to perfection.

The children returned into the house with great enthusiasm. "Are the brownies ready to eat, mom?"

"Yes, they are children." She directed them to take a seat while she placed a plate in front of each.

Suddenly, the mother confessed she had a small bit of news to share with the children. She told them this news was important for them to know before they began eating their treat.

"I just wanted to let you know, before you bite into your brownie, I added one more special ingredient, before I put them in the oven for baking."

Bewildered, the children thought: pecans, raisins, cashews, surely mom wouldn't have ruined them with one of these?

"All I did was go out into the back yard and find a little dog poop. Just a little, and added it into the brownie batter. Just a tea spoon full. Don't worry, it was just a very little bit, so it won't matter. I'm sure in comparison with all the other delicious ingredients we put in, you won't even notice the difference."

Moral of the story, just a little poop can spoil the whole recipe.

Just a little bit of something really bad can do a lot of damage.

Your life is no different. A little poison can kill you, a little bit of something dangerous, can make a whole lot of difference. A little bit of good, and a little bit of bad.

One of my previous cardiac surgeon customers, Dr. Bill Cohn, use to say it like this; "Bullets are small, but they can kill you!"

It is critically important for you to understand this fact. Why? Because what you expose your eyes and ears to, is entering your mind and has an effect on you. If you now realize how truly unique and precious you are, you won't want to throw the diamond of you into the mud, anymore.

"You can never learn less; you can only learn more." R. Buckminster Fuller

Are you empowered with enough healthy self love to take better care of yourself? Have you learned the importance of being more protective with what you say and do? Do you realize how important it is to determine who to allow or remove from taking time in your life?

You do not have to sabotage yourself to fail. You do not have to go to every fight you are invited to, or take the bait. You do not have to people please anyone you meet. You do not have to listen to junk, hang around junk, or buy junk, anymore.

"Nobody knows what you want except you. And nobody will be as sorry as you if you don't get it. Wanting some other way to live is proof enough of deserving it. Having it is hard work, but not having it is sheer hell." Lillian Hellman

If you want to be happy, you have to surround yourself with happiness, until it becomes your own. Consider the effort a spiritual blood transfusion.

Take sabotage, which is negative, and turn it upside down, and transform it into successful sabotage.

"How do I turn bad sabotage, into successful sabotage?"

Strategically place positive reading, writing and hearing, everywhere you know your mind, ears, and body will inevitably go. Remember, you're happiness is worth the effort!

When you take vitamins, do you take a bunch of vitamins in one day and expect them to give you a lifetime of positive results? When you go to the gym, do you lift weights once a month and expect to build solid muscles which last forever? Do you brush your teeth once a day and go the rest of your life feeling as if it is humiliating to ever brush them again? Do you find combing your hair more than once a day agony? When you water your plants, do you water them one time and say, "OK, I watered my plants, they never need watering again?" No, of course not.

Your ability to maintain positive thinking and your ability to maintain your inner happiness, requires the same consistent attention as all the other examples provided above. It is not only what you do, but also when and how much you do the right thing.

Reading helpful happy books, watching positive television shows, listening to uplifting radio programs, surfing the net for positive ideas, all these actions implant positive vitamins into your mind. You must take them, get them into your mind, allow them to transform your mind, and the happy result will naturally follow.

Every time you go to the positive resource gym, you are building happiness muscles. Any gym has many different types of fitness equipment machines to help you achieve overall healthy success. The same is true for your mind.

Does an athlete graduate from having to exercise? You don't hear people say, "I've graduated from having to take vitamins," or "I've graduated from having to go to the gym." Going to the gym, exercising, and taking vitamins is compounding interest in the saving account of you.

The more you do it, the better you feel, the more you enjoy the result, and the more you do what it takes to get those good results.

Happiness is an ongoing process that offers limitless benefits.

"Happiness is along the way, not at the end of the road, for then the journey is over, and it is too late. Today, this hour, this minute, is the day for each of us to sense the fact that life is good, with all its trials and troubles, and perhaps more interesting because of them." Robert R. Updegraff

Exposing your eyes, ears, and mind to positive sources of energy, equals an explosion of happiness and serenity. You can't even imagine how much happiness you can build, until you begin to try.

You may not have had a good mentor, good examples in the past, to teach you how to be happy. That was then; this is now. Surrounding yourself with transformation, involves immersing yourself in those good resources that provide good examples you can follow.

"The first great gift we can bestow on others is a good example." Thomas Morell

Remember the law of seed, time, and harvest? Plant a seed, give it time, a harvest will appear. Plant a good seed, give it time, be assured of a good harvest. Plant a bad seed, give it time, be assured of a bad harvest.

Good media tools carry DNA vitamins for happiness.

Over time, continuously ingesting these vitamins will produce a harvest full of happiness inside YOU.

If, then, happiness is something germinated from within yourself, in your own mind and heart, and not from a source outside yourself, then it stands to reason we have to get some happiness seeds inside of you to grow. How do we get those seeds of happiness inside you?

The answer is simple, the seeds are planted through what you read, see, and hear.

Eat an apple, get the vitamins and antioxidant benefits of what the apple offers, inside of you. The apple becomes part of you once you eat it. The same is true for happiness. We have to get you to eat the right happiness foods to keep your heart, soul, and mind, happy through what you see, read, and hear. Devour the good things you want to enjoy, just like your favorite desert treat!

The Eucharistic faith of the Catholic Church (www.catholicscomehome.org) has taught this idea for over two thousand years (STOP - this is a test of the emergency green sky and blue grass official system. Did you just go into defense mode when you read that last sentence, OR did you implement the law of no, and self adjust your station to thinking? "I might not know what I don't know about this," calmly). Ok, now that the surprise self exam of progress has been injected for your personal reflection, here is the rest of the story.

Catholics believe the second person of the Holy Trinity, Jesus himself, is truly transformed from the wine, water, and visible bread, during the consecration, into His body and blood; the Eucharist.

If God is love, and Christ is God, then receiving communion allows us to connect with this genuine love in a living manner. Not just in thought, but deed. Now that's a whole lot of love!

"If God could make the world out of nothing; He can certainly make something (himself) out of something (bread and wine)." Fr. John Corapi (www.ewtn.com)

"What and where are these resource stores that offer happiness DNA seeds for my soul?" You've wasted a lot of time going to the hardware store for bread in the past, don't waste time trying to buy good seeds from the store marked bad seeds supplied here.

Do you want to know where the good DNA seeds, those healthy media tools, can be found?

This is just a short list of media tools you can surround yourself with to help achieve transformation of any bad, into many blessings.

- Books
- Mini Books
- E-Books
- Periodicals
- CD's/Tapes
- Mp 3 talks/Twitter
- Radio
- Television
- Internet
- Blogs
- Movies
- Phone Teleconferences
- Retreats
- Seminars

Have you noticed web links throughout the book, and positive quotes from people who have already walked the talk?

These were deliberately placed here for you, to help you continue using this book as a resource guide towards your happiness.

A variety packed tool box, including a map you can always open when you feel lost. A guide to help you find your way back onto the right happy track, a transformation machine turning your green sky to blue, blue grass to green, upside down, into right side up. For this, I certainly pray.

What are airplanes built to do? They are built to fly in the air. Do they ever need to refuel on the ground or land to pick up passengers?

You are built for flying too, for getting off the blue grass, away from the green clouds. You are transforming your mind with these media tools into the blue clouds of happiness, over the rolling green hills of gratitude. Where do you land? Happiness Island, with shimmering oceans of optimism, miles of serenity sand, healing rays of warm sun, the sound of self love, the knowledge of being in God's tender loving care, the gentle breeze in the hope of a fresh new life. Don't you feel absolutely fabulous to be you?

Imagine this book is your landing location. You can rest a while here, recharge, and readjust your flight plan. You can always return the plane to home base for a tune up.

"A mind once stretched can never return to its original shape." Albert Einstein

When you learn a good habit, you practice getting good results. Success breeds success. Perhaps you fall down now and then; it does not matter! What matters is that you get up when you backslide, and move forward towards progress. Everyone backslides, don't be surprised when it happens, and don't beat yourself up when you fall. We all fall.

"If you should fall at times, don't become discouraged and stop striving to advance, for even from this fall, God will bring good." St. Teresa of Avila

Waves come up to the beach closer at high tide, and inevitably shrink back into the massive ocean at low tide. Do you find this natural event unnatural? Is the back and forth of the tide a surprise to you? Why then, would you worry about the ups and downs, the back and forth, the near and far, you might experience on this new path to happiness.

"Pray, hope, and don't worry." Padre Pio

One size does not fit all. There is something different for everyone to enjoy on the menu. No one wears the same size clothing, drives the same car models, and lives in the same style home. Nature itself does not produce just one breed of dogs. There are many leaves needed to properly create a tree. Enjoy being uniquely you; the difference is the delight.

"Character cannot be developed in ease and quiet. Only through experience of trial and suffering can the soul be strengthened, vision cleared, ambition inspired, and success achieved." Helen Keller

Surrounding yourself in positive transformation tools feeds your positive experiences. Learning from others is the only way to learn. Discovering who is teaching you how to become happier or more confused, is a new tool of preventative medicine.

Sabotage yourself for success!

"Sabotage," as defined by Webster's dictionary is, "a deliberate destruction of an employer's property or hindering of production by workers. Destructive or hampering action by enemy agents or sympathizers in time of war."

You are in a war for sure. The war is with you. You're fighting for your own happiness.

Turning sabotage upside down into successful sabotage is then a deliberate effort to set yourself up for happy success!

"How do I deliberately sabotage myself for success?"

Bombard yourself with the positive wherever you go. Place pictures, words, phrases, or even a statue or trinket, anything that reminds you of a goal that you want to achieve, in a location you are sure to see. Deliberately place a specific item, something you know ignites a positive focus, in a place that you can't avoid. This will force you, by association, to remember the positive thought and feeling you associate with this item. In other words, you are sabotaging yourself for happy success!

"If you concentrate on finding whatever is good in every situation, you will discover that your life will suddenly be filled with gratitude, a feeling that nurtures the soul." Rabbi Harold Kushner

How can you apply successful sabotage with media tools in your own life immediately?

Exercise:

Name seven things you always do in a day. Here are a few of mine to get you started. 1. Brush my teeth. 2. Make morning coffee. 3. Look at my calendar 4. Drive my car 5. Work on my computer 6. Watch TV. 7. Walk around my house.

Your turn;

List seven things you know you do each and every day.

1._____

2._____

3._____

4._____

5._____

6._____

7._____

Strategic sabotage involves placing something different in each of those seven locations that you know will automatically ignite a positive thought and feeling, enforcing a goal of happiness you are seeking to achieve.

How does this work?

In the morning, when I get up to brush my teeth, I automatically look in the mirror. So, the mirror is my unavoidable location where I start every day. That being said, I have placed two power cards, one by Louise Hay (www.louisehay.com), and one by Cheryl Richardson (www.cherylrichardson.com), which are taped to my mirror. I brush my teeth, I look at the mirror, I see the power cards, I read the message, I plant the happy seed, and the happy seed grows. I selected my favorite phrase, in my favorite color. These mirror messages are always changing, as I am changing.

Morning coffee is another must do ritual for me. I deliberately place a daily calendar near the coffee maker. A calendar that reflects a picture and phrase that keeps my mind anticipating something fantastically unexpected to happen during my day. A Flavia calendar, bible quotes calendar, or Cheryl Richardson calendar, there is always something new to discover.

Why do they all work together the same way?

These seeds of happy wisdom, by mentors who have achieved the dream, keep the focus on the positive possibility that happiness is just around the corner for you, too. The ten seconds it takes to read these quotes, delivers ten times more good lasting results to enjoy.

My daytime calendar is another frequently visited location. What do I need help with here? For me, having had to deal in the medical sales arena for over twenty years, daily life could be rather stressful, not only because of the sales elements, but because dealing with a multitude of different types of people in the cardiac surgery arena exposed me to a large spectrum of different types of people and personalities. Everyone had a different agenda.

Choices.

I needed to focus on the things I could control, not the things outside my control. I strategically placed a few powerful phrases inside my daytime pages, which I knew in advance that I would have to see as I planned and booked appointments throughout the day. Some of my phrases included, "Don't spend $200.00 dollars of your energy on a $2.00 problem," "Pain is inevitable, suffering is optional." "For with God, nothing will be impossible." "One day at a time." "The road to success is always under construction." "Dream." "Fear is useless, what is needed is trust." These are healthy "hooks" to refocus my mind and attitude towards more productive pastures.

What about driving my car? I know I am confined for a bit of time here, so I try to prompt myself to utilize this time wisely. First, I remind myself to pray by keeping a very small photo of the blessed mother of God near my Altoids® mints in the dash. (Okay, I know you're laughing at me, but I'm confident the blessed mother is not insulted about sharing space with my breath mints, if her picture helps to freshen up my mind with thoughts of God.)

I remind myself to listen to motivational CD's and tapes by keeping them within arms reach on the passenger seat. Dead space in the car does not have to be dead space in my head. I have a large collection of spiritual and motivational talks to keep me focused on the positive.

My key chain? Another great must see car tool, which for me includes a small photo of Medjurgorje, Yugoslavia, a cross my hairdresser's daughter picked out for me for my birthday, and my Regis College tag.

What do these three things represent for me?

The Medjugorje charm reminds me of a place I visited in 1990, where I was more peaceful than I have ever been in my life. The cross from Kelsey reminds me to reflect on how important it is to keep the mind of child, overwhelmed a child of six would deliberately pick out such a profound gift for me. The Regis College charm always reminds me of how good it feels to learn and participate, as I reflect on the variety of courses I enjoyed during that time in my life, and how happy I felt when participating in such solid camaraderie of many swim team experiences there.

Sometimes we need to remind ourselves of the good things from our past, to help fuel the dream for something even better in our future. This is what successful sabotage tools do for me.

Do you work at your computer? I do. What do I do to successfully sabotage myself here? I sign up for daily inspirational quotes, which keep me focused on my God who is bigger than my problems. The word of God everyday (www.wordofgodeveryday.com) or insights for your day by Bob Proctor (www.insightfortheday.com).

In addition, I successfully sabotage what is around my computer as well. A small figurine of a diva chick looking in the mirror printed with the words, "It's not the age, it's the attitude," to remind me I'm never too old to make a difference.

A colorful greeting card framed on my filing cabinet reads, "Promise yourself to reach for your stars, be the best you can be, find joy in each day, share your gifts with the world, live every moment with all your heart." What could be more to the positive point than that?

A ninety nine cent globe pencil sharpener keeps my frame of mind beyond this small space in which I live. Seeing that enormity of the world forces me to remember there are millions of people walking this earth, in this very moment, in need of something, or someone. A prayer of humility connects us all in a positive worth much more than the ninety nine cent item that ignited the thought.

What about television? I find positive shows to watch that teach me good lessons. I enjoy EWTN and Daystar. In addition, I have placed statues and photos that remind me of God's love for me, realities that help me grow honesty, integrity, enthusiasm, and love. It's impossible to avoid, and that's the whole idea.

How much time do you spend in your house? A lot! Here is a place where you can be really creative. Just as we frame pictures of the special places we've been, or the people we care about, to remind ourselves of those good times, we can frame the special goals in our life we want to keep.

The title of a book, *Do It Now*, stands perched beside my CD player, and reminds me to stop procrastinating when the inevitable urge may strike. A picture of Christ in the hallway, engaging in conversation with the little children, reminds me of a gentle, approachable god who loved children so deeply, God is no one to ever fear. An angel above a doorway brings comfort. I feel watched over, and cared for, by the power of spiritual love.

All these many things are alive to me, in my heart when I see them; I am inspired with right side up, hopeful thoughts. These good thoughts generate good feelings, peaceful feelings. They give me reminders of hope. Hope always motivates me to keep on going on. The quest to live a right side up world, and share anything of value that I can, is a reminder I never want to forget.

Make where you live a haven for happiness, and design a home with meaning and purpose. You're alive living in there, so make it come alive for you too!

"Nine tenths of education is encouragement." Anatole France

Successful sabotage is encouraging your education in the school of happiness. If you enjoy the bible, create successful sabotage scriptures and post them all over your house, in your car, in your checkbook, hide them in your shoes. Be creative and have fun with this effort.

"People rarely succeed unless they have fun in what they are doing." Dale Carnegie

Your journey to turn your upside world right side up, is a journey to love yourself. You can't love yourself until you believed you are loved, and loveable.

"God is perfectly good. His nature is unchangeable, supreme dignity. Superabundant love, an inexhaustible treasure." St Basil

Seeing the good in the bad is a new language for you.

How do you learn a new language?

You have to learn the letter, properly enunciate, and start with small phrases. Later, phrases become sentences, then conversations. Eventually, you are able to think in the new language without having to stop and translate. The more you use the language, the easier and more natural it is to speak.

Disciplining yourself to use this new language every day, gives you a freedom to utilize the language more efficiently to your benefit. You are perhaps willing to make some mistakes, a word, a tense out of place, and still persevere in your endeavor to learn. You understand the mistakes go along with the process of learning to speak in a new way. You might even laugh at yourself during those moments of error, because you accept it's just part of the process of learning the language. Mistakes do not stop you from achieving your ultimate goal to speak the language fluently.

How dedicated to learning this language are you?

If you really want to accelerate the process, you even may move to the country that has this language as their primary communication. As you are constantly immersed in the language, hearing, seeing, and speaking it yourself, you are being transformed to understand the language better. You are learning much easier, more quickly, and having more fun learning this way!

You want to be happy. You do not want happiness to be your second language; you always want to use it as your first. You want to learn it in a solid way; you can speak it forever, wherever you go. This is what surrounding yourself with happy media tools will do for you.

Surrounding yourself with positive media tools will help you speak happy language easily. Reading positive books, listening to encouraging seminars or retreats on CD's, find inspiring television shows to watch, listening to inspirational radio, find encouraging blogs, websites, and articles on the Internet to read, will accomplish this goal. Write your favorite positive inspirational quotes and tape them to your mirror, refrigerator, on your coffee pot, in your car, hide them as a surprise gift for yourself in your bureau drawer. Be creative and have fun!

Sabotaging yourself for success is like bringing the new language of the country to you, instead of you going to the country.

All of these tools are going to help you learn the language quicker, so it can become your own to speak fluently. The more you use it, the better you get at it. The better you get at it, the more you can enjoy the benefits of being able to use it. Isn't that the whole point?

When you know and understand the language yourself, you don't have to be afraid of being stranded alone in some far off corner of the country with no one to help you get home. You have yourself to rely on, because you carry the ability to communicate the right words, at the right time, in the right context, at any given moment. You have the confidence that you can handle anything unexpected with your skill of fluent language, to be comfortable that you can deal successfully with any situation that comes your way.

Learn the language of happiness. Wherever you go, there you are, as happy, and peaceful, as you could ever hope to be.

Carry your own light and you'll never have to depend on borrowing another's. You will have the tools to extinguish the darkness, and transform your space into light. You have nothing to fear, you can see your life right side up now.

"Nothing in life is to be feared. It is only to be understood." Marie Curie

Surround yourself in a different happy media tool once a day, to learn, understand, and be comfortable speaking in happiness. Begin now.

Imagine every unique media tool is an acorn you can plant to grow happiness in your happy tree of life. How much happiness can you grow surrounding yourself constantly with these positive media tools?

"The creation of a thousand forests is in one acorn." Ralph Waldo Emerson

CHAPTER VII

ENOUGH ABOUT YOU - VOLUNTEERING

"He who throws black pitch at another, keeps some stuck to his own hands first." The Bible

You get to keep what ever you give away, good or bad, in this life. If you think volunteering is designed to help another person, you are wrong. That is upside down thinking. In a right side up world, you are wise and understand the person getting most of the help from you're volunteering, is YOU.

"I'll be greedy, selfish, and nasty to everyone I meet, all day long. In return, God, the Universe, My Higher Power, will reward me with peace, prosperity, and happiness, all the days of my life?" How upside down a thought is that?

Does gravity fall up?

No, you most assuredly must give away what you want, in order to receive it back to you.

This fact is NOT a secret. It is simple, obvious, and easy to do. You can not think of peace, serenity, and Happy Island when your fists are clenched tight for a fight. The two contradictory ideas can not maintain the same space.

Green Sky and Blue Grass will only change if you have the tool to transplant truthful vision in your mind.

If you throw fresh juicy manure at a person, what happens to you?

You have quite a bit of that smelly, disgusting, undesirable manure remaining on your own hands. What you threw at them ultimately remained on you. The same is true for volunteering. Throwing kindness, generosity, and fragrant acts of love, will give you back each of these in abundance.

Volunteering or giving away your time, treasure, and talents, does not rob you of time, energy, or money. That is green sky thinking. True blue thinking understands that giving all of these freely away is a guarantee to receive more of each.

"Before we can give love away, we must know we are loved. To share joy, we need to have the experience of joy and delight within our soul. For peace and patience to flower, we must be patient and accepting of others, and ourselves. The unparalleled gift of kindness is nurtured by gentleness, and generosity of thought, and deed." Pegge Bernecher

Webster's Dictionary defines volunteering as, "To offer or give voluntarily; Synonymous with an exercise of free will, deliberate and unforced."

Imagine volunteering as an action that says, "I love you," to the whole world.

What could be more of an act of your free will, or unforced, than loving someone in action without expecting anything in return? Your unselfish thought, transformed into action towards another without words, is saying, "I love you."

"Loves very nature is to give and want the best for the beloved. Love gives for no other motive than to cause the other person to grow and be all that God created them to be. Love desires the total and complete freedom of the beloved. Love says I not only want the best for you, I have to do whatever I can to help bring that about. Love says I'm interested in you for your sake alone." Fr. Emmerich Vogt (www.12-step-review.org)

What happens if you hold a gun to someone's head and force them to say, "I love you?" Do you think they sincerely do love you with free will, or do you think they are saying whatever you want them to say because you are holding a gun to their head?

The words, "I love you," does not always make it so.

Love is a verb, an action word, not a passive thought. Love is not something you coerce or manipulate; it originates from within the very depth of your soul and the core of who you are. It is without question the greatest gift of being alive. In fact, nothing can make you feel more alive than knowing you are truly loved, and accepted, exactly as you are.

Do you have to be the person you want to attract? If the answer is yes, then you must give love first, before you can ever expect to receive it.

Volunteering, giving the love you have to the world, invites the whole world to love you back. WOW! Now that's a lot of love! The best news is, if someone doesn't accept your love (better known as rejection); you just get all that love back to keep. Nothing is ever wasted. You can recycle your volunteer happiness somewhere, with someone else, beginning with you.

How could this be true?

Imagine you go out and buy someone a beautiful gift. You wrap it up fabulously, put a magnificent bow on the box, and then give it to that special someone. What has to happen next in order for that gift to be fully given?

First, you have to get the gift, and then you must give the gift. But, the final step is most assuredly out of your control. The most important part of the gift giving process has absolutely nothing to do with you. It rests solely on the other person. The other person has to accept your gift to finalize the gift giving process. The transaction from you to them must occur; otherwise, you're left standing at the party with a gift in your hand and no one to take it.

The key for you to remember is that if the other person does not accept your gift, you just get to keep it for yourself. You haven't lost the gift; it continues to belong to you if not accepted by another. What choice do you have now? You might decide to keep it for yourself, or give it to someone else who will enjoy and appreciate it all the more. The choice is now yours. You always have choices in a right side up world.

Volunteering is just like that gift giving process.

You have a gift to give away, your time, treasure, or talents. Perhaps some people won't like, or accept your gift, so what! The gift is not wasted, because someone else will most assuredly be grateful that the other person's loss is now their gain. A person who does not accept you gift has nothing to do with you, it has everything to do with them. They are demonstrating ingratitude, arrogance, and selfishness.

What more can you do?

Send them a positive prayer. The refusal of the gift describes the inner condition of their soul, which is in a very sad state. Focus on the positive. Keep your eyes on the smiles of the people who love the gifts you give, can't thank you enough for them, and appreciate your thoughtfulness. Let go of the people who are blind. The best action you can do for them is to pray their heart will change into humble love.

"Many people have a wrong idea of what constitutes true happiness. It is not attained through self gratification, but through fidelity to a worthy purpose." Helen Keller

Make your purpose to help other people find their purpose. This is a worthy cause God will always reward. God is never outdone in generosity.

"You must give in order to receive, is the most right side up thinking you could integrate into the fabric of your being. It is a sure way to achieve and maintain your own permanent happiness." Fr. Benedict Groeschel (www.ewtn.com/tv/prime_sunday.asp)

A psychologist and priest in the Bronx of New York City, Fr. Benedict describes one of the most powerful remedies to becoming healthier is to, "get out of yourself and help someone else."

What else does volunteering do to help YOU be happier?

The fact that you are helping someone else be happy reinforces the love, and happiness in you. You are reinforcing the good healthy lessons you've already learned here. You are cementing the lessons you are attempting to learn better.

Have you ever had to teach someone something?

Your child, a colleague, or friend? Did you realize in the process of teaching that you were actually learning more yourself? Did you discover that you did not truly understand what it is you were teaching, until you actually had to teach someone?

The same is true for your peace and happiness. The more you volunteer and give to others what you have learned, the more you understand and appreciate your ownership of what it is you're trying to give away. This is genuine upside down, turned right side up!

Consider the fact that you will have fun doing this volunteering. What could be more fun than fun? Doesn't fun make you feel happy? The smile on the face of another looking into your eyes must bring a smile to your own face.

"The kinder and more thoughtful a person is, the more kindness they can find in other people." Leo Tolstoy

- Do you ever imagine what you will leave behind when you die?
- Do you ever reflect if you will accomplish your life's purpose?
- Do you know in this moment that there is something you have been called to do, but have procrastinated beginning?

You have been created for a specific purpose, and you will never be fully happy until you live this purpose. When something is doing what it is designed for, fluidity follows. This natural happy process occurs effortlessly, without resistance. Dr. Wayne Dyer would call this, *The Power of Intention*.

Have you ever heard, "Don't try to put a square peg in a round hole?"

That ease of the square peg fitting in the square hole is sure success. The square is where it belongs; it's in the right place. That success, fitting into the right place, is easy to accomplish. When does the struggle occur? The frustration happens when you try to force the square peg in the round hole. Why? The square peg was not designed to fit in the round hole. The round pegs were designed to fit in the round hole. Who is making the error? The square peg, the round peg, or you, for trying to put something where you know it does not belong?

Making a difference in the life of someone else in a positive way is a purpose you are predestined to achieve. You are a unique, unrepeatable person; your gift to give is also unique and unrepeatable. Living your purpose of making a positive difference in the world will automatically bring you happiness.

Volunteering your specific time, treasure, and talents is like **The Starfish Story**.

"Along the coast of the vast Atlantic ocean there lived a young boy. Each day when the tide went out, he would make his way along the beach for miles. An old man who lived not far away would occasionally watch as the young boy vanished into the distance and later noticed that he had returned. The neighbor also noticed that as he walked, the young child would often stoop down to lift something from the sand and toss it away into the water.

One day, when the child went down to the beach, this neighbor followed to satisfy his curiosity and, sure enough, as he watched, the young boy bent down and gently lifted something from the sand and threw it into the ocean. By the time the young child made his next stop, the old man had come near enough to see that he was picking up a starfish that had been stranded by the retreating tide and would, of course, die of dehydration before the tide returned. As the young boy turned to return it to the ocean, the old man called out with a degree of mockery in his voice, "Hey, young boy! What are you doing? This beach goes on for hundreds of miles, and thousands of starfish get washed up every day! Surely you don't think that throwing a few back in is going to matter?"

The young boy listened and paused for a moment, then held the starfish in his hand out toward the old man and quietly spoke, "Well, it matters to this one." Author Unknown

If you're the one out of a million who is diagnosed with a rare incurable cancer, the odds of getting cancer do not matter to you. You have cancer, and that makes the odds of you getting it one hundred percent.

In the same way, the person receiving your gift is on the one hundred percent program.

When you give your gift of happiness to someone, anyone, that makes your gift one hundred percent for them. Every time you give something good away from the depth of your heart, with sincere motivation, you are giving something even better back to yourself. One more good seed planted in your garden of life. One more facet cut in the brilliant diamond of you. One more healing sunrise at peace beach.

"You give little when you give of your possessions. It is when you give of yourself that you truly give." Kahil Gibran

"OK, Deb, I'm beginning to buy into this volunteering thing having some personal worth, but what type of volunteering would I do? When would I find the time to do it? I have a high pressure job, a husband, a wife, I travel for work, the dog and cat have to be walked and fed, along with the kids! Where will I find the time?"

Good news for you!

Your definition of volunteering being synonymous with quantity, and enormous amounts of time and energy, is upside down.

The truthful right side up thinking, demonstrates volunteering can be as much, or as little as you want it to be. The most important requirement in volunteering successfully, hinges on the genuineness of how you give away whatever it is that uniquely and creatively trademarks you as the gift.

"We can not do great things; we can only do small things with great love." St. Theresa the Little Flower of Liseaux

Whenever you give away your time, treasure, or talent, you have successfully volunteered. You can freely give anything of yourself away, expecting nothing in return. A smile, a consoling word, a prayer, are all free gifts in the world economy, and priceless treasures in the spiritual economy.

You must have open arms to take hold of any gift, an open heart, and open mind. Right side up thinking accepts that you must first let go of something to be able to receive. Upside down thinking stubbornly insists that you hold on to something, before you ever are willing to let it go.

Greed is a green sky, with rolling hills of blue grass to no where. Volunteering is the antidote to the disease of greed, so prevalent in sorrowful souls today. Be the antidote by your example, and others will follow when they see you being and doing, happy.

"The smallest act of kindness is worth more than the grandest intention." Oscar Wilde

Visualize each act of volunteering as spreading millions of happiness seeds all over the world and in your garden of life. Unexpected fields of every color, shape, and size are going to grow, which you may never know about. Does it matter?

What matters to you is the knowledge your acts of volunteering will grow into something beautiful, productive, and worthwhile. Your unique talents and skills will explode over time, once you set them free. Seeds in a package, hidden in your kitchen drawer do no good. You must get them into some soil for them to take root. Plant your seeds of self and watch your happiness grow as big as the bold blue sky.

"I think I began learning long ago that those who are the happiest people, are those who do the most for others." Booker T. Washington

Why is volunteering an easy, natural act for you to do?

Just like the flower has been designed and created to develop seeds which blow in the wind to bring beauty to new areas of soil, your talents and skills must be volunteered away in order for you to be fully beautiful and alive. Unique talents and skills you have developed over time will not remain contained inside your heart. Like a volcano ready to erupt, you must release these to be completely free. You must let them go in order to make room for the new things God desires you to posses. You must give in order to receive. You will receive deep happiness in volunteering.

"Believe me; I tell you the truth, there is more joy in giving than in receiving." Jesus

Ready for some fun, easy, and specific volunteer tips?

Do you have one of those daily motivational calendars on your desk yet? What do you do with that page of wisdom at the end of the day? Do you simply rip it off the cardboard, throw away the wisdom, anxiously anticipating tomorrow's thought for the day? What if you shared this happy, positive thought with someone else? How might you share this knowledge? Perhaps you could cut out the message, tape it to the back of your bills, a friend's card, or onto a box you are sending for work? Why not "volunteer" that piece of inspiration you enjoyed from your calendar, and give it away to the postman, the woman opening up the electric bills, anyone who may come across your letter, or package? What about giving that message to the person who receives the package at work, and all the many people who handle the package along the way of getting that package to the intended recipient? How many good seeds have you recycled and planted now?

Start turning that upside down thinking lie that you don't have the time, energy, or money, to volunteer right down the toilet. It's wrong thinking it is! I tell you, it's wrong! There are millions of ways for you to volunteer quite effectively every single day, for virtually no money, or time. Let go of that upside down belief that because it's small, it doesn't matter.

If every single person in the United States of America gave you a small fifty cent donation, believe me, you'd be one of the richest people in the world. Your opinion of doing something small and insignificant is based on the world's philosophy. You must transform, translate the notion that volunteering is not worth doing, if it is not done in large quantity.

Remember, if you're the one starfish that just was put back in the water, the rescue matters to you - big time.

What types of volunteering might you try then?

What are your talents?

I happen to love color and wrapping gifts. In my career as a cardiothoracic specialist, I often shipped equipment and product to operating rooms for unexpected surgeries, or inevitable ordering glitches.

I can remember one occasion where Michael Layne from the operating room at Brigham and Women's Hospital, called me because he was in a jam and needed a beating heart surgery item for Dr. Aranki. Now, I could have just put the product in the FedEx® package as all the times before, or I could have volunteered some sunshine into the effort.

How? Well, I just took out my leopard wrapping paper, and decked up that product with a glamorous matching leopard bow before placing it in the box, and shipped it off with some personal Deb style! A few extra minutes, some fun at my end, and a simple monotonous routine event to open an ordinary FedEx® package, became a major event of laughter and fun conversation to this very day.

The extra ten minutes it took me to wrap that gift, created an immortal smile of sunshine. The ordinary became the extraordinary. That boring day suddenly had something fun and interesting spiced up into it. The day was a little happier and fun for everyone. The problem of needing a product became a gift to receive some unexpected happiness.

The product was exactly the same, but the message attached to it through the pretty wrapping effort said, "You're special; I care." Isn't that what volunteering is all about?

Do you like to bake? Try out a new recipe and bring it down to your fire department or local police station. Do you like to talk? Tell someone you think they look nice, you appreciate them being in your life, offer to share a piece of wisdom you recently learned. Do you like to write? Send someone a thank you note that you never wrote before, and take the time to write a hello. Send a thank you note to a soldier in Iraq or Afghanistan. Do you like to shop? Offer to pick up some needed items for your local church or women's crisis center. Do you enjoy the elderly? Take a little time to go up to an old age home and listen to someone share their life story with you. Do you like to garden? Pick some flowers from your garden and bring them up to the waiting room in your local hospital. Do you like animals? Volunteer at your local animal shelter to visit the lonely cats and dogs. Do you like to read good motivational books or magazines? Bring your out-dated material to share with folks at your gym, doctor's office, or nail/hair salon. You don't have any time or talent at all? Then say a prayer for the lonely, depressed, or those about to die, and ask God to bless them with His peace and love. Add happy spice to someone's life, and you'll taste how flavorful your life can be.

You are encouraged to volunteer in the bigger, stereotypical ways if you are able. You have no excuse not to volunteer at all. The spiritual economy does not judge the value of your effort by the quantity of the effort as the world does. The spiritual economy sets the value of your action by your motivation. The very fact that you are acting to do something without expecting anything in return, gives the action its value. Give solely for the sake of giving.

The sincerity and love with which you do the giving is what brings value to the giving.

Your life is between you and your God. His opinion is the only one that matters anyway. What people think, or say, or feel, is irrelevant in this matter.

Consider the story of the widow's mite. The Lord said the widow contributed the least amount of money with only two coins, but He also said she contributed the most. How could this be?

She gave the most, because she gave everything she had to give. The genuine love with which she gave the little bit she had, made it more valuable than the people who gave excess monetary millions. She gave millions in love, sincerity, and right side up motivation. She gave from her heart, and expected nothing in return.

"Be joyful and happy; for this is the true mark of the Spirit of God who wished that we should serve Him in peace and contentment."
St. Margaret Mary Alacoque

It is impossible to be depressed, to have anger turned inward, when you are volunteering away a talent out of love to another person. Just as it is impossible to have light and dark in the same space, you are unable to be angry and bitter when you volunteer love.

Make a deliberate choice to volunteer and you have automatically made a deliberate choice to be happy and to free yourself from being unhappy.

Volunteering is a sure way to enjoy lasting victory in your life, and one of the easiest most natural guarantees towards being hugged by happiness.

Matthew Kelly (www.matthewkelly.org) asks us the question, "What are you doing with your life?" Doing is an action word, which demands we put our belief of who we are, and why we are here, into something more tangible beyond a thought, or a word, or a philosophical premise.

We must DO something to show what it is we believe, think, and feel. Volunteering is the easiest way to prove you are not lying when you say your existence on this earth is to make a positive difference.

Exercise:

Fill in the blanks with the first word that comes to your mind.

1. I have the motivation to accomplish_____.
2. I have the talent to contribute_____.
3. I desire to achieve the result of_____.

List a motivation you have, a talent, and a good result the combination can achieve. For example, my motivation is to please God, my talent may be to talk a lot, my result may be to apply my motivation and talent to help teenagers desire closeness with God. This makes me happy.

Now your turn:

My motivation of_____, combined with my talent

of, _____, results in

_____. This equation combination makes me happy.

Your motivation is the key to creating any value, good or bad; to whatever it is you are doing. Your motivation is the sincerity behind the effort and what makes it legitimate or fake. Your motivation is what gives you peace of mind, or fear, and anxiety behind the task at hand. There is nothing more important to your Higher Power than your motivation.

Volunteering is a great way to enforce the discipline of learning honorable intentions, and helping you enjoy right side up motivations as well. Why?

Because the very nature of volunteering attaches with it the end result of expecting nothing in return.

Expecting nothing in return most assuredly purifies your intentions. The ultimate irony of course, the upside down flavor to the whole process, is that it does give you something in return. The greatest gift you receive is your own happiness, a lasting happiness. Not for a day, a month, or a year. It is an integrity, an honorable quality that you weave into the fabric of who you are, guaranteeing you will never be, or see, life in the same way again.

Seth Godin (www.sethgodin.com) is a famous, well respected, leader in the marketing industry. He is also a very gifted engaging speaker. He is able to communicate to audiences in a fresh new way.

Having met him, I had the opportunity to ask him a question. I had only one. "Where did you learn how to be such a great speaker?"

He responded without hesitation, "Summer camp with kids."

Perhaps bewildered, the word ran out of my mouth before I could grab it, "What?"

Again, he stated, "summer camp with kids." He then clarified: in his younger years he volunteered teaching kids how to canoe during summer camp.

"When you have to keep a huge group of kids engaged on learning how to canoe, you learn creative ways to keep them focused when you talk."

No expensive courses, intricate classes, or fancy conferences, Seth Godin was just going about his life, doing something he enjoyed. Using all the creative talents God gave him, Seth made the effort to do what he wanted to accomplish better. His sincerity to help the kids was out of personal care, not money.

This is where the story turns. Seth Godin volunteering this action in the past, to give away his knowledge and enthusiasm, ironically is the very gift that has helped transform him into one of the most successful, and well respected individuals in the marketing industry today.

So I ask you. Did he lose by giving to those kids?

Did he get more than he could ever ask or imagine in the end? Do you think that during summer camp he was motivated to get a multi-million dollar return for his volunteering? What motivated him to help those summer camp kids learn how to canoe? Did he do it for his own personal gain, or to freely help the kids? You be the judge.

Once you begin to enjoy the rich rewards of volunteering, these habits naturally evolve into more good actions. These habits are not forced or coerced, they are enjoyable experiences which you begin to desire and want to maintain for your inner happiness. An acquired taste at first, becomes you're standard main course meal. Happiness you carry wherever we go, because wherever you go, there you are.

"Give what you have to someone; it may be better than you dare to think." Henry Wadsworth Longfellow

Building a habit of volunteering each and every day with a word of encouragement, a smile of acceptance, a seed of healing through the people we meet, the mail we send, the actions we engage in at home or at work, is a promise for inner peace.

Do you not like yourself enough not to want to have peace and happiness? Why would you deny yourself the opportunity to feel good about yourself when you can achieve this for free?

Why do you believe the lies that have been told to you that because something doesn't cost a green dollar bill it has no value? Why don't you listen to your own gut instinct that convinces you that you haven't been happy doing what you've been doing, and it's about time you threw that foolish notion far away?

Make your new vision of success, right side up. Take yourself to task, and prove it to yourself by engaging in this simple philosophy for being happy. The worst that could happen is that you made a few other people happier, and the best that could happen is that you made yourself happier. How is that for a good investment?

"We are what we repeatedly do. Excellence, then, is not an act, but a habit." Aristotle

Repeatedly build good volunteering habits, and you will find fruits of happiness grow.

Do you like people who cheat, steel, are lazy, and lie?

Do you want to have friends like that? Do you admire or respect those types of people? How would you feel if your children hung out with people like that? How do you feel when I describe someone like that: a cheater, a liar, a lazy irresponsible person who strives to take advantage of any one, a real user, professional self centered opportunist, and con-artist? Do you care about someone who is nice to you only because they want something from you, today or tomorrow? Most assuredly ending with, "You owe me one."

Do you admire or respect a person like that? Do you want that type of person to be your friend? Do you want to be like that person? What if I said YOU were that person I just described? How do you feel now?

Every time you lie, cheat, or steal, you send yourself the message that you despise yourself. You send the message to yourself that you can't stand you, and that's a very bad place to be. You must first be proud of yourself, happy with yourself, love yourself in a healthy way, before you can attract happy people who are happy with themselves into your life.

You must be the person you want to attract.

You can design yourself into a fabulous creation through volunteering. It is a quick, easy, and fun way to transform your upside down world, right side up, in some big or small way, everyday.

"To love oneself is the beginning of a life long romance." Oscar Wilde

How do you learn to love yourself in this upside down world of a selfish, all about me show existence?

Green sky, upside down thinking believes the more I keep for myself, the more powerful, and safe I will become. Blue sky, right side up thinking believes, the more I give, the more abundance I will receive. If you do not want to stay stuck with the results offered by the all about me show, you have to change the channel to the all about you show, and volunteer.

"The harder one grips, the faster it slips through one finger." Alan Watts

You might think you are holding on to something of value by not volunteering, but the reality is exactly opposite. It is in the letting go, which allows you to accomplish what you truly want. You will be happier, faster, in a lasting way.

Volunteering is humility that has been crystallized. Humility is the number one character trait of truly successful, happy, and peaceful people.

Humility is not thinking less of oneself, it is thinking about oneself less.

Don't be selfish with yourself; the world needs you.

If you plant hope, volunteer something in this present moment, you will bloom healthy happiness. Incorporate that spirit of volunteering into who you are, and in whatever you are already doing. Sometimes it's not doing something different, it's simply doing it differently that makes all the difference.

Perhaps your personal style does not include leopard wrapping paper, but you too, can add some volunteering color to everything you do. Wrap your unique talent in some fun way, and give it away, as fast as you can. Turn your upside down world, right side up, by volunteering the diamond of you.

"I will either find a way, or make one." Latin Proverb

For more fun, easy, quick volunteer tips for everyone, go to my website, www.2minutevolunteer.com, and be sure to add your own creative volunteer tip too!

CHAPTER VIII

IMMERSE YOURSELF IN TRANSFORMATION - SEMINARS AND RETREATS

"Every living thing loves its own kind, every man like himself. Every being is drawn to its own kind; with his own kind every man associates. Is a wolf ever allied with a lamb?" The Bible

You are whom you associate with.

In the same way you learned the new accent in your new language of happiness, you will immerse yourself in transformation through happy focused seminars and retreats, which will accelerate your own internal happiness. High dose vitamins to energize your healthy new mind!

"The mind grows by what it feeds on." Josiah G. Holland

You need to feed on happy ideas, through peaceful happy people, to think in new happier ways. Situations do not always change immediately, but you can change in this very moment.

"How can participating, or attending a seminar or retreat accelerate my ability to achieve the happiness I seek?"

Do you have a favorite sport?

Do you like to watch this professional sport on television? Perhaps football, baseball, or basketball? How do you feel when you watch the game at home?

Now, compare this experience, of watching the game on your television set alone at home, with physically going to the stadium of where your favorite game is being televised? How do you feel now? What is the difference you experience being surrounded by hundreds of fans in the stands? The sounds you hear of cheering, the celebration you see of fans standing up celebrating victory, the energy of everyone focused on the same desire for your team to win. How does it all feel in every sense you possess?

You can watch the game at home, or you can go to the stadium.

You still see the same game, but the experience is completely different. Which one has more impact? Which one resonates stronger with you? Which one offers you the full experience of the game? Which one do you remember more passionately? Which one is more fun to attend?

Seminars and retreats will turn your upside down world, right side up, fast. Why?

Because you are surrounding yourself with a number of other people, committed to the same goal as you, who possess the passion and purpose to want to achieve the same goal as you. What you learn there is more than knowledge. The experience of being immersed in the effort is a gift itself. The people you meet, the stories you share, the hope you can't buy. This is a powerful oasis of happiness!

"The people you spend time with absolutely makes a difference in your life by directly affecting your ability to be happy." Bill O'Reilly

You may be saying, "I don't need to take the time to go to a retreat or seminar to be truly happy." I agree. You may not have to go to your son or daughter's birthday party, a formal religious event, mass, wedding, or your parents twenty-fifth wedding anniversary. You can always send a card. You do have to attend each event to receive the maximum benefit of the event. You do have to participate and be present to gain the full experience of the event.

No, you don't have to go physically to any of these things to be thought of there. You do have to go the event to experience the maximum benefit the celebration has to offer you, and the others around you.

Attending seminars and retreats is like being surrounded by a group of people wearing your favorite perfume or cologne. You never spray any of it directly on yourself, but somehow you come home with the fragrance lingering on your clothes anyway.

The focus, and energy delivered in seminars and retreats is like taking concentrated healthy mind vitamins, and being hosed down with your favorite fragrance, all at the same time.

These environments carry you towards your goal almost effortlessly. Just as the wind easily carries a fallen leaf wherever the wind takes it, you will be carried to destination happiness through the energy of the people around you wanting to get there as well.

Did you ever have to write a paper for a course you took in high school or college? How did you accomplish this goal? First, you had to attend the class. Then, you had to listen to an instructor that obviously knew more than you on the subject matter. Next, you had to decide on a topic to write about. Once you made that decision, you needed to find good material related to the subject you selected, to engage in good research. You had to concentrate your time and energy to investigate the information you gathered, and select the most important pieces from that information to utilize in your paper. Once you accomplished this step, you wrote the paper as well as you were able. You might have asked a friend to proof read it for structure and content, before you were completely satisfied with the quality of your work. Finally, you submitted the work to your teacher for critique and final grading. What did your final grade reflect? Your final grade was probably a good reflection of the time, energy, and effort you dedicated to the project.

"When the time to perform arrives, the time to prepare has past." Unknown

Going to seminars and retreats is similar to writing your paper. There is one important difference. In attending seminars and retreats, the grade is the gift, your gift of being happy.

You first have decide to be happy. Then you have to decide what is blocking your ability to be happy, where to learn how to replace your unhappiness with happiness, and investigate further. Once you decide on the tools to use to build your happiness, you need to find and get good material. This good material includes participating in seminars and retreats.

While you are participating in these seminars and retreats, you are taking the time, energy and focus to assimilate the subject matter at hand. You are writing the paper of your life story, and how you will now be acting in it. The grade, the gift at the end of the effort, is a measure of the peace, and happiness you keep. The amount of peace and happiness you receive will also be a good reflection of the amount of time, energy, and effort you expended throughout the seminar or retreat.

Seminars and retreats can be local, far away, a day, a week, and anything in between. The goal is to decide, in advance, what it is you want to receive.

My personal experience is that people don't so much have a problem attending a seminar or retreat, as much as knowing how to select which type is right for them.

- How do you decide which seminar and retreat to attend?
- How will you know which one is right for you?
- How will you find the seminar and retreat that will be most helpful for you?

First, we need to say a prayer for you. "God, I am so grateful that I'm starting to truly like myself and enjoy my own company. I know you want me to love myself in a healthy way, and I'm trying to do the right things to get there. You created me for a specific purpose, during this time of world history, and I'm asking you to help me know what my purpose is. Lead me, put a desire in my heart, show me now what type of things I need to do and attend to help me be stronger, more self-assured, peaceful, happier, about being the best person I was created to be. Help me to be happy, happiness that only you can show me how to keep and enjoy. Lead me to happiness where no one can steal my joy. Thank you very much for loving me just the way I am, but loving me too much to let me stay that way. Amen."

Great!

Now you merely have to keep an open heart and mind, believing God will always answer a prayer like that. Remember, you don't know what you don't know, so let go of any expectation of how the answer may arrive, you only have to believe that it will.

One day, in a one moment, you will be reading something, listening to someone, or seeing something that says, "Wow! I've just got to check out attending this event." Your heart will beat faster, energy will rise in your blood, and the knowledge that this event is for you will bring you inner peace.

Let me share an example of how I arrived at one of my first retreats in Medjugorje, Yugoslavia, in 1990.

Back in 1989, my dad was diagnosed with cardiac disease and required a double bypass heart surgery. Having been in the medical sales profession since I graduated from college in 1984, I was rather worry free of the routine nature of the procedure. I had observed numerous cardiac bypass procedures with grafts (CABG's), and certainly didn't foresee any complications here, with only two grafts.

My assumption proved wrong. What happened during that event, radically changed life for my entire family forever; mom, dad, nana, and me.

I met with the surgeon after dad's surgery.

"Everything went just fine, Deb, completely routine."

Later in the evening, the unexpected call came from the attending surgeon, "You and your mom better come into the hospital right away. Your father's heart has fibrillated, and I'm not sure he's going to make it through the night."

Surreal, devastated, my own heart shrunk into nonexistence. Denial, disbelief, numbness ran through my veins, and words could not move out of my brain.

Mom was still at work, and my grandmother (my mother's mother, who lived with us since I was six) was sitting at the kitchen table when I got the call. Realizing something was dreadfully wrong, I slurred a short phrase to inform her of the news.

"We must pray," and out came her rosary.

My grandmother was an old French Canadian jewel. Filled with faith, hope, and trust in God, she was a serious prayer warrior. Every type of prayer, in any place, at any time, for any reason, thanking or asking.

Growing up, I perhaps never completely agreed with the concept of a loving God, or faith, but I was certainly listening to her now. Tragedy and crisis have a way of doing that to you.

Dad and me, we never had what I would consider a close relationship growing up, perhaps not unlike your own paternal relationship. In this moment of disaster, it didn't seem to matter. What suddenly did matter was the unexpected regret that overwhelmed me with uncontrollable fear and guilt. I would give anything in my world to have more time to repair all damage. Time to say, "I'm sorry," time to say, "thank you," time to say, "I love you."

Snatched, like a sudden earthquake, everything in my life was different, upside down. Helpless and out of control, I was totally powerless to do anything to change the situation.

My dad, in the intensive care unit that evening, quickly had the wires cut in his chest, exposing his naked heart. The chief cardiac fellow held my dad's heart in his own bare hands, providing the necessary heart massage to keep his blood flow pumping.

By the time my mom and me were allowed to see him, the fluid retained in his body from the lack of circulation had exploded.

Dad's bodily size expanded like the Good Year blimp, he was nearly unrecognizable. He was alive, but he certainly didn't know it.

What followed during the course of the next three weeks was one worse day after another. One more hurdle, one more obstacle, one more piece of information that was more horrid than the last. His lungs had collapsed (tension pneumothorax), and later both went into acute respiratory distress. Lungs in acute respiratory distress mean they are so stiff they could explode. This demanded maintenance on a respirator to prevent them from doing just that, exploding. The reaction to the enormous amount of drugs constantly pumped into his system caused his skin to begin peeling off his whole body like the shedding of a snake. Eventually, pneumonia set in with infectious debris. His sternum (chest) was left open with only gauze sponges to cover his internal organs and beating heart. This situation caused dad to come down with mediastinitus, a deadly infection of the sternum bone. Scraping, and removing the bone (the big one you feel down the middle of your chest) and replacing the space with another bodily muscle, was the only clinical solution. Tissue from his stomach was removed, and replaced to his chest to hold him together. Kidneys began to fail, forcing dialysis machine treatments. For his own safety, the doctors maintained him on a drug that induced paralysis, so he couldn't even blink his eyes. Unconscious throughout the entire event, doctors were not hopeful he would ever wake up without brain damage.

Every day, when this rapidly sliding scale of news got worse, my mom would tell me to pray, and offer something special to God to help my dad live. She consistently encouraged me to return to the church. Convinced God wanted me to be close to Him again in receiving communion.

Daily trips to the hospital in Boston were dreadful. We never knew what terrible information would be hitting us next.

With much time alone with mom, we talked, and talked, and talked. Despite my argument praying to a God I was not sure existed was the ultimate hypocrisy, she never stopped telling me to offer a sacrifice to God, tell him I would return to the sacraments.

"Tell God you will go back to Mass and receive communion for one year. God wants nothing more than to have you receive communion." Day after day, she asked me to do the same thing, and day after day I told her "no" because it was all a bunch of nonsense.

After three weeks of this daily sinking from worse, to more worse, to even worse than that, the doctor called with that hesitating, sterile voice, that always precedes bad news. This was the grand finale; the end of hope had arrived.

"Your dad isn't releasing carbon dioxide any more Deb, there's just nothing else we can do. I'm sorry."

That phone hit the receiver with an echoing ache that brought me to my knees. Every ounce of life was drained right out of me. We had come so far, how could this be happening now? The tears flooded out of me, and in that one moment, I knew I had to put my pride aside, and promise what my mom had been asking.

Words weren't needed for that prayer, although I said them through a drenched face and gasping breath. My heart was already bleeding the words right out of my soul.

"Please God, if you exist, please let my dad live. Please let him be okay. If it's truly important to you, like my mom says, if it matters, I'll go to church and receive communion every week for a year."

The pain of loosing my dad, in that very specific moment of helplessness, was greater than my personal pride and fear of hypocrisy. It was a distasteful bargain with a God that I didn't really know, or was not sure existed. I didn't care. It was a promise to do something I had never done, and didn't believe mattered. But, in the end, that prayer changed all our lives for the better.

The hospital staff was mystified when we got there. Dad's vital signs started turning around. He suddenly was able to release carbon dioxide. He was suddenly in stable condition.

Who was more surprised than anyone? Me. But not my mom. She just looked into my eyes, and asked, "Why did it take you so long to make that promise I told you to offer weeks ago."

Dad went in for surgery early November of 1989, and didn't come home until March of the following year. It was a long haul, and in the beginning, when he regained consciousness, he could only move his thumb. From there, he needed to learn how to walk all over again in Spaulding Rehab. Yes indeed, it was a very long and slow journey.

Years later, I can still see my dad outside riding his lawn mower, complaining about all the yard work that he has to do. Giving my mom heck, for buying another tree to be planted.

None of these memories would have been possible, within any reach, if not for a living God. A God who sometimes has to resort to making a miracle out of a mess, because we won't talk to Him, or listen to Him, in any other way.

During the time my dad was still in the hospital, I remember hearing about a place called Medjugorje (www.medjugorje.org).

Similar to Fatima or Lourdes, although the apparitions of Our Lady had not been officially church approved at that time. Open to learn and curious to discover anything that would help me understand what or who this God was, this Medjogorje piqued my interest.

Searching to learn anything more about this place and what was happening there, I found little to satisfy my appetite. One piece of information led to another, then another. Specifically working to find a Medjugorje newsletter I had learned about during my quest. One contact after another, led to another organization, until someone gave me an actual phone number of someone to call who may have had it.

Barbara was her name, and when I explained how I arrived at calling her, asking if she had a copy of this newsletter, I was unprepared for her response.

"Well, I don't have the newspaper, but I am organizing a group to go to Medjugorje in May."

"What?!?" I thought she was crazy.

"No, you don't understand. I have no interest to make a trip to Yugoslavia; I just want to find the paper and read more about the story."

She asked for my address, and promised to send me whatever she could find.

When the package finally arrived, I was excited to see the return address was from Barbara.

"Hey mom, I think that lady found the newsletter I wanted." Nana and mom sat around the kitchen table, excited to see the contents. What fell out of the little brown envelope was far from my newsletter. A tiny hand made, purple rosary, with a note from Barbara, "These rosaries were blessed during one of the Medjugorje apparitions. I thought you should have them. Included is the information on our pilgrimage to Yugoslavia in May."

Have you ever had a hit you in the head like a ton of bricks feeling?

A feeling in the depth of your gut that something was meant to be, whether you liked it or not? This was one of those moments for me. The last thing I wanted to do was trek off to Yugoslavia with a bunch of Holy Roller people I never met. Neither did I want to go to an apparition site with the mother of the God, when I was just beginning to accept the idea of her son. Shouldn't I spend a bit more time concentrating on Christ before I started trying to meet the other family members? This was all a bit too much for me to digest, and quite honestly, I worked hard to dismiss the notion. I didn't even know how to say a rosary!

I did go to Medjugorje, and the real miracle is that my mom and dad drove me to the bus to send me on my way. My dad, unconscious through most of his trauma, was overwhelmed and dumbfounded about this radical change in his all too rebellious, know it all daughter. Did he try to talk me out of going? You bet not! The fact that he was still above ground functioning was enough evidence for him.

I was in Medjugorje one week. One week that changed every other day for the rest of my life. Peaceful, positive, powerful. Unexpected miracles in every one I met, in every way I felt, where ever I went. Peace, peace, and more peace. Surrounded by people who were searching for the same. A gift that no amount of money could buy.

Was life a bed of roses after that retreat?

No, in fact there were many more challenges. There still are today. The difference is the peace, the faith, the trust, that does not change like the deepest part of an ocean. The anchor of awareness there is a God, a Higher Power, greater than any problem on earth, brings a measure of happiness that God will always bring something good out of something bad, keeps the world right side up.

If you want to learn more about the messages of Medjugorje, I would suggest the book, *Queen of the Cosmos*, by Jan Connell.

I wasn't planning to go on retreat to Medjugorje in my wildest dream. I had no intention or desire, but somehow it came to me.

You too, have a story waiting for you, one specifically designed to help you become the best person you were created to be. Find a retreat or seminar that will instill the steadfast happiness into your life you most desire.

As the four minute mile story goes, you won't know how fast you can truly run, until someone else shows you how it's already been done.

Get yourself to a seminar and/or retreat, and surround yourself with four minute mile runners. It will make possibility, a tangible reality. If it is possible for them, it is possible for you. Deliberately place yourself in an environment that helps you believe it is true for you.

Aren't you worth the effort?

"All who have accomplished great things have had a great aim; have fixed their gaze on a goal which was high, one which sometimes seemed impossible." Orison Swett Marden

The goal may seem too high for you to immerse yourself in the transformation a seminar or retreat can offer you, but you are worth the effort!

Go to a motivational seminar, go on a Crisio, and participate in free programs at your local church, synagogue, or mosque. Most of the quotes I have included in the book have web links next to them. Most of these people offer seminars or retreats. A few hours, a day, or a week. Know that whatever you decide to do, it is going to plant huge amounts of good seed packages into your life, for the rest of your life.

Just like those perennial plants that come up year, after year, after year without you needing to do a thing to make them multiply and grow, know beyond any doubt that your seminar/retreat experience will continue to bring you fresh flowers of happiness every year, for the rest of your whole entire life. Now that's a good right side up reason to be happy!

"Faith is knowing there is an ocean because you have seen a brook." William Arthur Ward

The experience has to become your own to be real. You can read and listen to another person's story, but until you have the experience yourself, you can not truly understand the transformation it can bring you.

Do you know how an orange tastes because someone told you? Or do you know the true flavor of the orange because you tasted the orange yourself? Going to a seminar or retreat will turn your upside down world, right side up. The experience will change the color of your sky and the rolling hills under your feet. Nothing will be the same. It will all be much better.

"We enjoy faith in the good times, and exercise it in the bad." Mother Angelica (www.ewtn.com)

Trust your own good intuition that you've been feeling hope as you journey through the words in this book. I know you do! The little moments of "WOW! What if it is true? What if I can be happy? What if it all does work?"

"Fear is useless, what is needed is trust." Jesus

Fear is a tragic disease.

Fear never brings you anything healthy, unless it happens to warn you to keep your hand off the red hot stove or away from a train wreck. Fear, the type of fear that lies to you about not being good enough, or lovable enough, or the lie that you could never be genuinely happy, is the spirit of fear I'm talking about. Valuable energy wasted. Replace your fear with trust, and surround yourself with people who have put that belief into action.

The easiest way to hold tight to that good spirit of trust, is to get around people who are looking for it, have it, and want to get more of it with you. Those people are in seminars and retreats, and you need to meet them! You need to get what they have, and in return, I'm sure you will volunteer a special gift to them in return, as well.

You are not finished yet.

Keep an open mind as to how your life story continues, and ends.

"Good to begin well, better to end well." Chinese Proverb

Are you afraid or embarrassed to attend a retreat or seminar?

Are you afraid or embarrassed to call the automobile club when your car battery dies, and you need to be towed? Are you ashamed to have jumper cables attached to your battery to recharge the system? Of course not!

You need help to get some energy into the battery of your mind, so it can work well again, too. You need the energy to get you the happiness you seek. To travel to peace beach, live under the healing sun.

Living that upside down life has drained you of a lot of precious energy, you have been running on fumes. A good powerful charge will get you moving strong again. Seminars and retreats will do this for you. There is nothing to apologize for in that.

Have you ever heard of Immacule Ilbegez (www.immaculee. com)?

I have attended two of her talks, watched her interviewed on television, listened to her cd's, and read her books. When I am inclined to have myself a pity party, I often think of sitting in my seminar seat, listening to her words, seeing her facial expressions, feeling her many deep authentic living emotions. It helps me get over myself fast.

Immaculee is a survivor, one of the few survivors from the genocide, and Rwanda Holocaust in Africa. She had no idea that it was coming, and thought the sequence of events that brought her home (because everyone at her school was slaughtered) was just a coincidence. At least at that time.

She found herself in a small little bathroom with nine other girls for three months in total isolation and silence. Outside those four small walls, her entire world was being destroyed. Her mother, father, brothers, family, friends, slaughtered and massacred with machete knives. Death by the thousands awaited her in the streets.

What kept her alive?

Faith, trust, forgiveness, hope. You can read her story for yourself and decide, *Left To Tell*.

Is your day ever that bad? Are you being held hostage in a bathroom for three months like Immacule? Is your entire family being brutally murdered outside your door? Are you feeling helpless or hopeless? Do you think you can never forgive again? Do you wonder how any good could come out of such horrible evil?

The world needs good mentors.

People who prove by example positive change is possible. You can find these people who have turned the upside down world, right side up in a variety of seminars and retreats. These people prove, and teach us, we are wrong that life can't be better. We may not always get what we want, but we can always get what we need.

"The truth without love is unbearable; love without the truth is a lie." Edith Stein

If you genuinely love yourself, you'll want the truth. It's a natural consequence of getting right side up. It is a gentle flowing, steady stream of attraction, to all things true.

"The enemy, evil, the devil, tears the truth apart, twist and manipulates truth, and turns it upside down, so he can destroy us." Fr. Wade Menezes (www.fathersofmercy.com)

When the sky is feeling green, run as fast as you can in the opposite direction! There is definitely a war out there, and you don't need to be one of the living dead casualties anymore.

While my mother was going through her cancer treatments at Mass General, my dad was in the same hospital for Stephen Johnson Syndrome, (he survived aortic aneurysm surgery, carotid artery surgery, a pacemaker implant, congestive heart failure, hernia surgery, all after the bypass surgery trauma. Hence, he earned the nickname in town of, Fred from the dead).

Mom was doing relatively well with her chemo treatments, and dad was not ill when I had decided to go on retreat to hear Fr. Emmerich Vogt. He was speaking on spirituality of the twelve steps in Birmingham, Alabama. I firmly believed I was going to a section of EWTN, only to discover I was actually going to Casa Maria Retreat House (www.sisterservants.org). This convent was next to, and worked in tandem with EWTN.

With dad now in the hospital again, as the only child care giver, the weekend retreat seemed irresponsible to attend. Of course, my mother disagreed.

On the way out of Mass General with mom in the car, my cell phone rings.

This soft spoken woman with a slight New York City accent politely stated, "I'm looking for Deb Scott please."

"Yes, this is Deb."

"This is Sr. Louise Marie Deb, from Casa Maria Retreat House in Birmingham, Alabama. I'm calling because we just had a room open up, and I thought you might want to take it for the retreat with Fr. Emmerich Vogt."

Oh no! My internal conversation was racing now – I was going to cancel the whole trip and suddenly this nun destructs my entire plan by telling me she now has a room available. What's up with that?

Mom, overhearing everything on speaker phone, chimed right in, and emphatically injected, I was absolutely going. Mom always took these coincidences as signs from God. If the room was now available, it was meant to be.

"Yes, yes, Sr. Louise, thank you, I'll take it."

Reluctantly leaving my mom for the weekend in the middle of her cancer treatments, with my dad still in the hospital battling his illness, not to mention my own back injury, I trekked off alone to my Alabama retreat.

The sisters and Fr. Lambert have become a second family over the years. They are tangible evidence of unconditional love, prayer support, and laughter. I never tire of visiting them, or leaving with the gift of hope they graciously offer.

Mom passed in February of 2005. Dad went soon after her, the following year in May of 2006. Nana had passed away in my arms years before. Yes, everyone is gone now, but somehow mom and God knew I needed to go on that retreat to find a second family, despite every reasonable fact that would have suggested otherwise. You don't know what you don't know!

"Courage is more exhilarating than fear, and in the long run it is easier. We do not have to become heroes over night. Just a step at a time, meeting each thing that comes up, seeing it not as dreadful as it appears, discovering we have the strength to stare it down." Eleanor Roosevelt

What could be more exciting than discovering who you were truly meant to be?

Discover your unique talents and use them wisely. Watch your happy seeds grow, and enjoy the pleasant surprise of observing all the beautiful shapes, sizes, and colors coming into happy full bloom.

Your life is no longer in black and white. You are the happy star in living color!

Seminars and retreats will help you be free to be the happy person you were created to be. Not the person everyone else wants you to be. There is nothing more exciting than creating, and discovering yourself.

Find a retreat to attend, and sign up now.

"You may delay, but time will not." Benjamin Franklin

CHAPTER IX

THE MAN/WOMAN AT THE TOP OF THE MOUNTAIN DIDN'T JUST HAPPEN TO FALL THERE!

"What I began by reading, I must finish by acting." Henry David Thoreau

- Do you think the person standing at the top of the mountain just happened to get there by spontaneously falling out of the sky?
- Do you think the Olympic gold medalist just happened to win the prize without practice?
- Do you think your perpetual happiness will be maintained without any effort from you?

Your commitment to turn your upside down world, right side up, is a choice available to you in every moment of your life. Green skies and blue grass are not true, unless you want them to be.

"If we open a quarrel between the past and the present, we shall find we have lost the future." Winston Churchill

You can have a happier today, and tomorrow, only when you make peace with all the good and bad events of your past. You can now transform the bad into good, and enjoy the benefits of all the events in your life to create a greater good. Nothing is ever wasted.

"We are all in the gutter, but some of us are looking up at the stars." Oscar Wilde

No human being is more special than any other. No one is without a problem, a worry, a fear. You are not alone in your struggle to turn your world right side up. You may, however, be one of the few who has the courage and desire to turn your upside down world right side up.

Struggles transformed into success, can create a new, and happier life for you. Transformation is permanent. The butterfly does not have the ability to return to its caterpillar suit, the forty-five year old can never be twelve again, and when you evaporate your green sky to blue, the world will be right side up for you.

Consider the **The Butterfly Story.**

"A man found the cocoon of a butterfly. One day a small opening appeared. He sat and watched the butterfly for several hours as it struggled to force its body through the little hole. Then it seemed to stop making any progress. It appeared as if it had gotten as far as it could, and it could go no further.

So to help the butterfly, he took a pair of scissors and snipped off the remaining bit of the cocoon. The butterfly then emerged easily. But it had a swollen body and small, shriveled wings. The man continued to watch the butterfly because he expected that, at any moment, the wings would enlarge and expand to be able to support the body, which would contract in time. Neither happened!

In fact, the butterfly spent the rest of its life crawling around with a swollen body and shriveled wings. It never was able to fly.

What the man, in his kindness and haste, did not understand was that the restricting cocoon and the struggle required for the butterfly to get through the tiny opening, was God's way of forcing fluid from the body of the butterfly into it wings, so that it would be ready for flight once it achieved its freedom from the cocoon". Author Unknown

Sometimes, the struggle is exactly what we need to be completely free. Be grateful for the stock pile of manure from your past, it is giving you the opportunity to achieve through transformation an equal amount of rich fertilizer. Rich fertilizer helps a bountiful garden grow large, lush, and strong.

"One of the greatest benefits of struggle is that it forces us to move when we would otherwise stand still. This leads to the full realization that success comes only through struggle. Show me a successful person, and I will show you someone who has struggled in life." Solomon Benard

You do not always have to understand why things happen the way they do, but you can always believe something good will be born out of them, in the end.

"God alone knows the secret plan of the things he will do for the world using my hand." Toyohiko Kagawa

Perceptions and feelings don't make anything a definitive truth. This is upside down thinking that no longer serves your achieving peace, purpose, and happiness.

Do not cling to the green sky illusion of **The Helen Keller Syndrome.**

For many years, all the people in Helen's family thought she was stupid, and allowed her to act as an uncontrolled animal. If she was deaf and blind, then she must be stupid and shallow. But then Annie Sullivan came along, and with patience, love, discipline, and persistence, Annie was the tool God used to release the true person of Helen through sign language.

Who was Helen now?

She was the same person before she met Annie Sullivan as after, but she was different, and she never again went back to her old way of being. Today, we know Helen Keller as one of the brightest, deepest thinkers of all time. She changed history in a powerful way most of us can never imagine achieving.

Don't fall into the "Helen Keller Syndrome" and think you know what is going on, or not going on inside the heart and mind of another person just because you don't physically see what you believe the outward appearance should be.

"You may have a fresh start at any moment you choose, for this thing that we call 'failure' is not in the falling down, but in the staying down." Mary Pickford

Get up, and get into your life!

Believe you can transform ANYTHING in your life from bad into good, even death into a new type of life.

Death, into a new type of life?

When my mom, and best friend (Rachel) passed away in 2005, I was left dead with her. In the depth of pain, I never felt or saw anything good in her passing. I took comfort she was happier in heaven, than suffering the slow death of cancer eating away at her, but in the all about me show, I was left here alone, empty, without her.

Going through cleaning all her millions of things from fifty years of marriage to my dad (who passed away the following year in 2006), I cried at the thought all these "things" had a memory for my mom in them. They each told a unique story.

My dad, in his anger and fury wanted to throw the entire attic away in a dumpsite. That wasn't working for me, as you might imagine.

Alone in my tears of grief, surrounded by all my mom's treasures, I received an inspiration that her things could live on in others by creating a little shop with the name, "A Little Bit of Rachel - The Unique Vintage Boutique."

You can visit the blog with more stories, and photos at: www.alittlebitofrachel.com, or the on-line shop with a lot of her vintage treasures at: www.rachelgirl.com.

Well, when I ran downstairs to share with my dad my new found epiphany, he naturally told me point blank I was absolutely nuts. In fact, he resentfully retaliated with, "A little bit of Rachel, after what I've seen she stashed up in that attic, I would say it's more like a whole lot of #@!* of Rachel!"

What happened next?

I found a small place for a little shop off the beaten path in Newburyport, friends painted it, helped bring all of mom's things into it, and I created a sign with my mother's signature lasered into it. Just like she had newly created the store herself!

People came by just to see the place. Prices were cheap, it wasn't about the money, it was about keeping the happy memory of mom alive in others, through her clothes, and many vintage gems. Customers would buy coats, come back weeks later, and tell me, "I took Rachel to New York City with me last week - we had a blast!"

I have books filled with comments like that. Rachel went to Lebanon, Sweden, and England, just to name a few. Many more places than when she was here on earth. And everyone had a story to tell about the beautiful woman, who lived life to the fullest, when they received a compliment on their purchase.

Inspired by death?

Many I met were just inspired that a mother/daughter relationship could be so close, that this "A Little Bit of Rachel," even existed. Some mothers got hope of a better relationship with their daughters when they walked through those store doors. That was priceless.

I would like to think the death of my mom, was transformed into a new life of something even better, greater, larger than her physical life itself.

One day, as I sifted through her many collectibles, I found this poem she wrote to her mother, after she passed away. My Nana (Yvonne), her mother, died in my arms in 1995. This was the poem;

The true love of a mother is indispensable.
Like a rose in bloom,
Like the smell of spring,
Like the whiteness of snow.
The true love a mother is indispensable.

Like a new baby,
Like the very first step…
By Rachel Scott

Do not wait to say, "I love you." Do not wait to appreciate the unique people God has placed in your life. Don't wait!

Keep hope alive, that anything can be transformed into something good. Even death, into a new type of life.

The real miracle?

My dad use to come by and visit me in the shop everyday. I think he came to enjoy speaking with all the customers, sharing personal stories of Rachel, even more than me.

Give yourself the gift of an open mind, keep the focus on yourself, do some praying, attend a 12 step program, find a good therapist or coach if you like, listen to and watch and read positive messages, volunteer, attend seminars and retreats, practice successful sabotage daily.

Do these actions and you will automatically reap the reward of being at the top of your mountain. Your day of holding your flag of happiness will arrive just in time for you. Not one minute too early, or a second too late. Seed, time, and harvest, remember?

Author and celebrated speaker, T.D. Jakes (www.tdjakes.com), focuses an entire book on what it takes to get to the top of that mountain. He titles it, *Maximize the Moment*. He emphasizes that the moment is all we have, and what we do with the dash between our birth and death dates engraved on our tombstones, is all that really matters.

Moment by moment, minute by minute, day by day, is how we get to the top of that mountain. Persistence combined with faith is a winning equation for your happiness.

- Are you afraid to make a mistake?
- Is there such a thing as a mistake?
- Who is your authority for defining if, when, or how, you make a mistake?

There are plenty of people out there who want to be the thirteenth apostle, but God picked His twelve, which are already in the Bible. He did not pick anyone you know to be number thirteen in His book, so why should you let them have authority to write YOUR life book. You are not finished yet. You do not know if what you perceive to be a mistake is not actually a blessing.

"I have learned more from my mistakes than from my successes." Sir Humphrey Davy

Do you worry?

Worry is an indicator that you do not believe God is big enough to handle your problem. You do not trust your higher power when you worry. This is an indicator to do all those things you just read about in this book all the more passionately.

"Pray, hope and don't worry." Padre Pio

If you pray, you will have inside you the hope that only God, your Higher Power, can give you. If you have hope that God is all powerful, all knowing, and all loving for you, then you will not worry. Worry is a bad disease that you do not need, and will not have when your world is right side up. Worry only walks on the hills of blue grass.

"When the heart weeps for what it has lost, the spirit laughs for what it has found." Sufi Teaching

What if everything in your life was happening EXACTLY as it should be? How does that make you feel? What if there were no coincidences, but as Deepak Chopra claims, only God incidences?

A coincidence by definition is, "a synchronistic experience." The very fact that it's a coincidence indicates it is synchronized. Who is the author of synchronization? God. So, coincidences can be messages from God. This is why it is important to never ignore reflecting on a coincidence that pauses your heart. Use the opportunity to reflect on what God may be telling you.

Exercise:

What do you now know, that you did not know, before reading this book? If you can't list at least seven things, then I have failed you.

1._____

2._____

3._____

4._____

5._____

6._____

7._____

Knowing, and knowing how to do something, and being able to do it, are all different ingredients you need to have to be happy.

The Airplane Story illustrates this fact.

"There are two different people piloting two different planes. The tickets cost the same, the plane is the same make and design. They are virtually identical twins. One plane pilot has never flown a plane before, but he has read every book on the planet about flying them. The other plane pilot has never read a book about flying, but his dad taught him/her to fly since childhood and has flown more hours than any man alive. Which plane do you pick? What pilot do you want flying the plane with your life?" Anonymous

I think we both have the same answer, the person who had the experience of flying. It is the same answer for implementing these tools you have read about in all the previous pages. The cost of making the right choice is high; the price is your very life.

How much is your life worth to you?

Your happiness? Your peace? Your opportunity to live on purpose?

You may have had a rough start getting out of the gates. Okay. A lot of us did as well. It would be great to begin well, but it's better to end well. You can still achieve the dream!

"I might not be where I want to be, but thank God I'm not where I used to be!" Joyce Meyer

Having been in the operating room watching numerous cardiac surgery procedures during my medical device sales days, I can tell you one thing for sure, everyone's heart is beating the same color blood under the skin. We all share the same life experiences, and emotions in different colored wrapping paper.

Remember, "If you don't stand up for something, you will fall for everything." Anonymous

That is why you need to speak out loud a commitment to yourself that happiness is possible, WITH all the baggage and manure you define as impossible to remove or overcome. The right word to focus on is: TRANSFORM.

It is impossible to change the past, the wrongs unjustly done to you, the hurt, the pain, the disappointments, the bad decisions, the losses. You absolutely can not change your past. You can use all those past events, and transform those feelings, experiences, lessons, into something good, fruitful and beneficial in your today and tomorrow.

There is always a Good Friday before Easter Sunday in my calendar. Can't have one without the other, in that order.

We are all sitting in the same boat my fellow traveler.

I have my personal share of misery, nasty rotten people, and all that jazz that goes into the best selling hit song, "pity party people like me." That song is not playing on our radio station anymore; new updated "happy hits" have overtaken the airwaves.

Believe it and receive it.

Mother Theresa used to say a phrase I often repeat out loud, and it's quite simple. "I trust in Jesus' tender loving care for me." Even Mother Teresa had tough days.

What is your anticipated outcome of this story?

A young Italian cloistered nun from Ohio feels the inspiration to build a chapel in the Deep South. She has no money to pay for it. No education to construct it. No experience to manage it. Absolutely nothing but an inspiration to do it.

She follows through (years later), finds some land, and pays for it by making fishing lures with the other sisters. She then starts writing little spiritual booklets to answer the many questions she's now getting by loads of mail, and the sisters print them up themselves.

Eventually, her inspiration grows towards television media. What? This is a cloistered nun – she doesn't even own a TV!

The rest is history. Today, EWTN (www.ewtn.com), the eternal word television network, is the largest catholic television network in the world, centered in Birmingham, Alabama.

Reaching one hundred fifty million homes, in one hundred forty four countries, and translated into numerous languages, this inspirational programming is available to you twenty-four hours a day, seven days a week.

Did she ever doubt? Mother Angelica when asked why she admitted to having felt doubt in her stomach aches answered with confident humor, "Well, sometimes my stomach doesn't know how much faith I have in my head and heart".

If you want to learn more about the life story of Mother Angelica, visit (www.raymondarroyo.com).

Words have power, and it is imperative you speak out loud and hear yourself make this commitment to reach the top of the mountain of your happiness. Don't be making excuses to say it silently in your head. That doesn't count. You have to hear the words from your very own mouth to your very own ears to make the equation work.

So, repeat after me, and don't be shy;

"I am a lovable, wonderful human being, exactly as I am, with all the good and bad in my past. I commit right now to being the best person I was created to be, and I know I can, and will be happy despite any or all tragedies and misfortunes from my past. I know that each trouble has the potential to be transformed into my biggest blessing. A prison into a palace. God is with me, helping me, guiding me, to happiness every moment of every day of my life, because He loves me."

You may not feel you will get to the top of the mountain, or that you have the ability to get to the top of the mountain, or see yourself at the top of the mountain of happiness. None of your feelings has anything to do with whether you can get to the top of the mountain and attain the happiness you seek.

Feelings are not facts. A diamond is a diamond, is a diamond, even if it is thirty feet below the dirt in the ground you can't see.

No matter what you may think, the diamond is there. YOU are that diamond.

Ronald Reagan said, "Anyone can accomplish anything if you don't worry about who gets the credit," and the Berlin Wall came tumbling down, with Communism right along side.

If you can dream it, you can do it.

Never give up on your dream to see the world right side up, and be at peace.

"We are not troubled by the things, but by the opinions we have of the things." Epicteitus

It is possible for you to see and live in a right side up world, even if everyone around you is upside down.

Have you ever heard **The $20.00 Bill Story**?

"It was already a few minutes into class, and none of the students could understand the teachers delay. What in the heck was he doing up there fumbling around with his wallet? Didn't he know the bell had already rung? The kids thought maybe class would be canceled and they might escape having to turn in their homework assignment.

Suddenly, the teacher expressed a look of success as he pulled out a $20.00 dollar bill from his wallet. Calling the group to immediate attention, he asked the class "What do I have in my hand?"

Everyone in the class just looked at each other, wondering what insanity had overcome their instructor.

Quietly, one young girl replied, "a $20.00 dollar bill."

The teacher was satisfied with her response.

"And how much is this $20.00 bill worth young lady?"

The student, a little bewildered answered hesitantly, "$20.00 dollars?"

With a high degree of enthusiasm, the teacher yelled to the group, "That's exactly right young lady! Exactly right!"

Without further comment, the teacher crumpled up the same $20.00 dollar bill into a tiny ball, then he took it and threw it on the dirty dusty floor, and stepped all over it repeatedly. Had their teacher gone insane?

After a long pause, the instructor picked up the dirty, wrinkled $20.00 dollar bill, opened it up, and looking at the young girl once again asked, "and how much is it worth now?"

The student, quite afraid to answer his confusing request, but more afraid not to answer, broke the room silence as she whispered "$20.00 dollars?"

Enthusiasm once again overcame the teacher, "That's right, that's exactly right!"

"Do you see my point students? What I'm trying to teach you? Never forget this lesson. No matter how much dirt may fall on you in life or how many people may have stepped on you, or how crumpled or broken you may appear to be, no person or event can ever change the value of who you are inside. $20.00 is worth $20.00 is worth $20.00 no matter what, and young people, you are each worth a million. Don't forget it." Anonymous

You have to expect some good days, slow days, happy days, sad days, on your way to the top. It's inevitable, don't be surprised or discouraged, it's just bound to happen to all of us along the way. It's part of the process.

"Growing spiritually can be like a roller coaster ride. Take comfort in the knowledge that the way down is only preparation for the way up." Rabbi Nachman of Breslov

Endurance and perseverance are the two strong legs of patience.

"When all is breaking up, something new is breaking through." Cheryl Richardson (www.cherylrichardson.com)

Get into motion.

When a car is stopped, it is difficult to move the steering wheel, and the tires. The tires are stuck. But when you are in motion, moving along the highway, it is easy to turn the steering wheel and change the direction of the tires attached to the car. When the car is moving, it can take you to the destination of where you want to go. You need to keep moving in the direction towards happiness, in order to arrive at happiness.

Get yourself in motion, and the magic will begin to appear. The happiness you seek on peace beach will surround you everywhere you look. Even in the midst of an island storm; especially in the midst of the storm. Serenity sand is always beneath your feet.

What do you do now?

Write your story.

About what?

About turning YOUR upside down world, right side up.

You're the book alive!

Share with the world how YOU;

- Find ways to remember, you don't know what you don't know, and keep an open mind.
- How do you maintain conversations with your creator in prayer?
- What programs have you joined to not go it alone?
- How did you find a good healthy mentor, therapist, or coach?
- What types of positive media tools are you surrounding yourself with to keep you happy?

- Where, and in what unique ways are you volunteering your unique sparkle shine of talents to the world?
- What seminars and/or retreats have you immersed yourself in to help propel yourself towards happy transformation?
- What are you doing everyday to enjoy being at the top of your happy mountain, where the sky is true blue, and the grass is genuine emerald green?

You being happy are the living pages breathing gifts of life into everyone you meet. Gifts of inspiration, peaceful purpose, and hope. You are writing to the whole world through your every day existence, the powerful message that it IS possible to find the happiness they seek.

Be a HAPPY blessing to others, and surely YOU will be blessed with HAPPINESS!

God bless you,

Deb

Deb Wants To Hear From YOU!

Share YOUR story of turning your upside down world right side up, Green Sky to Blue, Blue Grass to Green, at: www. greenskyandlbuegrass.com

EPILOGUE

Eulogy Read by Deb, for Mom (Rachel)

I am overwhelmed with a passage in the gospel of John, which describes the first miracle of our lord, at the wedding at Cana. He surprisingly saved the best wine until the end, and my mother, like that fine wine, grew into the best person God created her to be with each passing year.

We are born, we live, and we die. The dash distinguishing her life on this earth seems so small to the world, but so large in my heart. My mother was a beautiful mother, but I tell you my greatest loss is that of my very best friend.

She taught me to live in the present moment, trust God even when I couldn't understand why He did the thing He did, and trust that He would make everything OK in the end. She taught me forgiveness, tolerance, and inspired me to be the best person God created me to be. She taught me that love was an action word that was expressed most beautifully by joyful sacrifice and humility.

Her patience and ability to love someone for their good, and minimize their faults was unfailing, day after day after day after day. Her heart was embraced with a spirit of gratitude for every kindness, towards every person she ever met in her life.

In her battle with cancer, many cancers, from rectal to liver, and the indignities she suffered with the pain of her vaginal cancer, the rashes from her chemotherapy that riddled her entire body with poison ivy like rashes, radiation burns, and all the rest, she fought. She fought for my dad and me. And when my dad almost died again this past summer (Fred from the dead, nicknamed by many since he returned from so many hopeless cases), she continued to take care of home and family with grace and a positive attitude. She sacrificed herself for me and my dad and her extended family and friends without hesitation.

My mom's heart was a wellspring of compassion. If you are here at this service, I would venture to say she has prayed especially for you. People she met, or only heard of being in need, she prayed for by name. She prayed with her heart, deep, sincere prayers. She loved the prayer of her rosary and meditating on the life of Jesus and Mary, towards the end of how it helped each of us to accept Gods will for our lives, believing He always knew what was best for us.

The essence of her spirit is best described in a gentle prayer we came across during one of our most joyful vacations together, my mom, dad and I in Quebec, Canada, where we celebrated her birthday and visited the birthplace of my grandmother (her mother), in St. Philip de Neri. I don't know exactly how to say it in French, but the English translation states, "I want to stay a child, because it's wonderful for each day to be discovered." Yes, this was my mother's mantra, to live each day in child like wonder of the gift of life. She fully enjoyed her life, from feeding her birds, cooking a gourmet meal for family and friends, or just going for a walk with Chloe (our dog). She loved it all, the travel, the day trips, the shopping excursions (especially Christmas Tree Shops), even the laundry was an act of love and happiness. She tirelessly listened to any problem I encountered (which were many), and had a magnificent way of ending every conversation with a spirit of hope.

I thank you mom for teaching me to feel deeply, to love deeply, to live deeply. You were the best mother anyone could ever dream to have, but most of all you were the best friend anyone could ever hope to have. I will always love you and miss you and appreciate the generous gift God gave me in everything about you.

Eulogy Read by Deb, for Dad (Fred)

We are given the biblical truth, "when a man dies, his life is revealed," from the book of Sirach, chapter 11, verse 26. It continues to tell us that we should "call no man happy before his death, for by how he ends, a man is known." I never knew how merciful these words would be when it came to my dad and me.

What many of you already know if you are here, is that my dad, Fred, was a successful, honest business man who cared deeply for the growth and well being of this community and all the people in it. I am so proud, as I reflect on those old newspaper clippings (my mom having saved each and every one of course), that from his youngest days to his last, he was always busy contributing something to some organization, getting things done. From class President in his High School, President of the J.C's, salesman of the year at Fenn Motors, Realtor of the year, International award winner for the J.C's, President of the NBPT Realtors, chamber of commerce, United Way, Boys Scouts, and his favorite was definitely being President of NAID. I can see him laughing in the Anna Jaques intensive care unit the first week of April when he was reading the copy of the newspaper article Pete Morse brought him up stating he was elected NAID Foundation Director while he was in the intensive care unit down in Florida this past February. He looked at me, handed me the article, and chuckled with a smile, "Can you believe that?"

What you may not know, is the greatest accomplishment of all occurred during his last few months on earth. Yes, the body of the man Fred Scott was at its lowest due to illness, 113 pounds to be exact, but his spirit, sense of humor, and love was strong enough to move the world. He was bound and determined to build up enough strength from his hospital and rehab discharge in Florida, to make it back home for our March 30th plane flight. Our walks out to the pool for him to do his kicking exercises, our trips to the Dairy Queen® for a thick chocolate milkshake, the time we spent together going to a car dealership where he was center of attention, story telling as only Fred could do in the most interesting and amusing historical way. What fun we had simply driving around Coco Beach and Satellite Beach, always teaching me something new about a bird, building or flower. He always kept his sense of humor, even when he lost a filling during one of our dinners together, he commented, "Well, this really is the vacation from hell, I lost my wedding ring and now I lost a filling too. Doesn't that just figure?" I think I laughed the most when one morning I heard him yelling, "Rachel, Rachel, help."

I found him fallen out of his bed on the floor. He just looked up at me and said, "Well, at least you know I'm still thinking about your mother!" In the simplest conversations about the variety of sea shells I kept collecting from long walks on the beach while he was napping, we had discovered something about each other that we had always known, and never known. And it would be just like my dad, "Fred from the dead," to finally get along with me, and then go and leave me to be with his Rachel.

My dad would want to thank all of you for giving and sharing his life with him and my mom, and would want you to take that part of him that was so good, and keep it going on. His work ethic, his honesty, his passions, and most of all his famous jokes collected from years of morning coffee with all his buddies at Taffies. He truly enjoyed each of you as individuals, and you can honor him best by doing the same.

Mark 12, verse 27 says, "He is the God of the living, not of the dead." You never stopped being my dad, protecting me, teaching me, showing me how to successfully survive in this world. Proverbs says, "let your father and mother have joy." You're together again now, mom and dad, just like you always wanted to be. I love you both so very, very much.

Breinigsville, PA USA
09 January 2010
230426BV00001B/49/P